Praise for *The Social Organization*

"A great read with real and practical solutions on how to innovate and incubate new ideas for growth, leveraging a new and exciting tool—social media. I am eager to put these practices into place at my organization."

—Russell Evans, Senior Vice President
of Marketing, Experian

"The Social Organization is a forward-thinking and thought-provoking book that provides insights on how organizations are leveraging social technologies to quicken the pace of innovation. The research and emerging practices of the new world of collaboration are extremely compelling. This is a must-read and great playbook for transformational IT leaders."

—Mike Goodwin, Senior Vice President and CIO,
Hallmark Cards, Inc.

"The Social Organization is an amazing book, takes away the fears to get started with social media, but takes away also false expectations about what social media can do for you. Whether you are a business enterprise or a community, it gives you a solid framework to start, guide, develop, and reshape your social media strategy and will help you avoid commonly observed pitfalls."

—Nuria Simo, CIO, Royal Frieslandcampina

THE SOCIAL
ORGANIZATION

OTHER BOOKS IN THE GARTNER, INC./HARVARD BUSINESS REVIEW PRESS SERIES

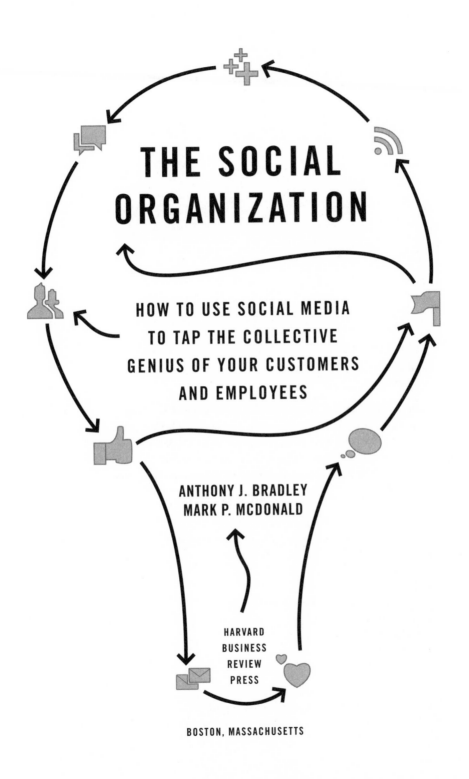

THE SOCIAL ORGANIZATION

HOW TO USE SOCIAL MEDIA
TO TAP THE COLLECTIVE
GENIUS OF YOUR CUSTOMERS
AND EMPLOYEES

ANTHONY J. BRADLEY
MARK P. MCDONALD

HARVARD
BUSINESS
REVIEW
PRESS

BOSTON, MASSACHUSETTS

Printed in the United States of America
10 9 8 7 6 5 4 3

Library of Congress Cataloging-in-Publication Data

Bradley, Anthony J.
      The social organization : how to use social media to tap the collective genius of your customers and employees / Anthony J. Bradley, Mark P. McDonald.
         p. cm.
      Includes index.
      ISBN 978-1-4221-7236-0 (alk. paper)
   1. Management—Social aspects.   2. Social media.   3. Industrial sociology.
   I. McDonald, Mark P., 1963-   II. Title.
      HD30.19.B73 2011
      658.8'72—dc23

                                                                    2011021190

The paper used in this publication meets the requirements of the American National Standard for Permanence of Paper for Publications and Documents in Libraries and Archives Z39.48-1992.

From Anthony J. Bradley
To my own little social structure—Renee,
Emmie, and Turin

From Mark P. McDonald
To my family, friends, and colleagues whose ideas,
energy, experience, and interest have been
inspirations for this book

CONTENTS

PREFACE

There are already many books available on social media technology and stories on how businesses are applying it. Undoubtedly there will be even more by the time you read this. So why write, or read, another?

Because despite the number of books published on social media, there is still a significant hole. And that is, how, as an organization, do you actually do it? How do you identify, catalyze, empower, and derive value from a community? How do you, as a leader and manager, help your organization build competency in using social media to foster productive collaboration—with your customers, your clients, your employees, and others along your value chain?

Answering these questions requires more than touting the latest technology or describing how you brought "Facebook, LinkedIn, YouTube, Twitter, and blogging" into your organization. Answering these questions and providing actionable advice for managers demands a full explanation of how organizations can generate collaboration on a massive scale, continuously guide that collaboration, and leverage it for business success.

There are whole sets of books that demonstrate the importance of social media with numerous short vignettes and that address subsets of the challenge like crowdsourcing and social media marketing.

This is a book dedicated to the bigger question of *how* to achieve broad and sustainable success, as an organization, using social media. It addresses the leadership, management, and operational capabilities you must build to achieve meaningful, repeatable, and significant business value with these powerful new technologies. We created this book based on extensive experience working with business leaders around the world and observing their social media successes and failures.

This book is not an introductory book on social media. It assumes you have a basic understanding of social media technology and its potential value and are now interested in strategically employing it for business value.

At Gartner we have had thousands of conversations with clients about how to select and employ social media technologies for business gain. In 2009 we began an extensive study of more than four hundred social media initiatives to further explore and analyze findings from our regular client interactions. This examination focused on answering two fundamental questions:

First, how are organizations using social media to deliver tangible and substantial business results?

Second, can we identify common practices that distinguish the successes from the failures?

Our study included organizations from around the world and across all major industries and assessed their different applications of social media. We focused on how "traditional" (in other words, non–Web-based) companies are using social media to create collaborative communities that include their customers and their employees. We intentionally avoided initiatives that used social media simply as additional marketing communication channels. It's not that social media communications aren't important to business. But much greater value comes from the mass collaboration—both inside and outside the enterprise—that social media technology now makes possible.

Our scope for the study was intentionally broad, but we also looked deeply into select organizations that were applying social media and mass collaboration more strategically with greater impact on their goals and operations. These deeper investigations looked at the issues facing organizations and their leaders, from how they guided mass collaboration, to how it was funded, measured, and coordinated within the organization.

We worked directly with organizations—facilitating strategy workshops, compiling detailed case studies, and consulting with company leaders who were directly involved in creating collaborative communities using social media. We believe these three layers—thousands of client interactions, hundreds of implementations analyzed, and a focused set of detailed examinations and direct collaboration with key leaders—provide a strong basis for our conclusions and recommendations.

Our overarching conclusion and the inspiration for the book is this:

Organizational success with social media is fundamentally a leadership and management challenge, not a technology implementation. Achieving that success creates mass collaboration that gives organizations unique capabilities to create value for customers, employees, and stakeholders.

This book is intended for business leaders and managers. Why? Because the extent to which an organization adopts and gains business value from social media is entirely up to them.

Specific social media tools and technologies will come and go. Web 2.0 will become Web 3.0, and the social media tech bubble may burst. But none of that matters as much as the intrinsic and sustainable value created when you become a highly collaborative social organization that can tap into the collective genius of your customers and employees.

Our goal is to provide you with the guidance, techniques, and tools to accelerate your progress and dramatically increase your chances of success in leading your company on its path to becoming a social organization.

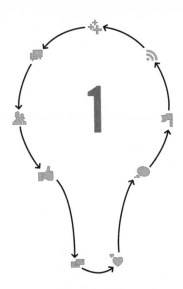

Introduction
The Promise of Social Organizations

W E ALL KNOW STORIES of start-ups that begin with a handful of people working together in one room, in daily contact with each other and with customers, users, suppliers, and anyone else important to their success. Everyone has a say in every major decision because the company can be run naturally as a collaborative enterprise.

But success brings growth, growth brings more people, and soon people have formal jobs with specific written duties and responsibilities. Before long, the company needs managers and hierarchy and departments full of specialists, along with processes for hiring, evaluating, planning, investing, and dozens of other "corporate" activities that require gigabytes of policies and procedures. Eventually, all that remains of those collaborative good old days, when everybody was in it together, are nostalgic stories told by the lucky few who were there.

Leaders have long recognized the penalties imposed by the increasing division of labor and specialization organizations require as they grow more complex. People's contributions are limited mostly to the areas where they work; and key players, like customers and prospects, are left out altogether.

Think of the possibilities, and the excitement, if your organization, like that start-up, could tap into the full talent, creativity, experience, and passion of all the people it touches—employees at all levels and locations, customers and prospects, and partners anywhere in your value chain. What if you could minimize the constraints imposed by specialization and compartmentalization? What if you could retain or recapture some of the benefits, human and organizational, of that collaborative start-up without losing the glue that currently holds the organization together?

That, in broad strokes, is the promise of social media. No wonder so many companies around the world are rushing to use it. Developed only in the past few years, social software is allowing what has never before been possible—the ability of vast numbers of people spread around the world to work together productively and to contribute the full range of their talent, creativity, and energy.

The hype is astounding, of course, but organizations today truly are entering one of those "For the first time in human history . . ." moments. Never before have hundreds, thousands—even millions—of people been able to simultaneously and collaboratively build massive documents, create huge content repositories, or make collective decisions. It is the scale of collaboration possible today—*mass* collaboration—that is new and transformational.

Since social media technology first appeared, we at Gartner have been studying how companies are applying it in their organizations and the results they're obtaining. We've had thousands of conversations and workshops with companies pursuing social media and have looked carefully at some four hundred implementations across industries worldwide. From that rich base, we have developed a good sense of where and for what purposes social media are being used.

One of our more striking discoveries is that most social media initiatives fail. Either they don't attract any interest or they never create business value. A key reason for failure is the host of misconceptions that have grown up in this area, many perpetuated by books and articles, that lead to ineffective practices. Key misconceptions include (but certainly aren't limited to):[1]

- *Social media doesn't deliver real business value and can waste a lot of employee time.* True, it *can* deliver little value and waste time, but not if you go about it the way we describe in this book.

- *Social media poses unacceptable risks to privacy, IP protection, regulatory compliance, HR infractions, customer service, and more.* Yes, but if done wrong, many things are risky. With social media, risks can be mitigated and managed.

- *Social media is just another marketing channel. Get a Facebook page, open a Twitter account, give your CEO a blog, and maybe load some cool videos on YouTube and you're done.* Not true. You'll need to do much more than that if you hope to capture its real potential.

- *All you need to do is provide social media technology and the rest will happen on its own. After all, that's how it happens on the Internet.* Wrong. This common approach is almost certain to fail. Success requires more than technology.

- *You don't need a business justification for social media because it's so cheap and you can't anticipate or measure the benefits anyway.* Not true. You *can* measure its benefits. And that's good, because it's more expensive than it appears and you'll need more than faith and high hopes to win the support of organizational leaders.

In the course of the book, we'll address all these dangerous misconceptions in detail and describe what you must do to avoid them. We know what's possible because we've learned that some companies do move beyond the hype and misconceptions to succeed. In fact, we've seen a few companies move far ahead of others in the widespread and effective use of these new technologies. They are using them to create substantial, tangible business value—in many cases value that couldn't be created any other way—and we are beginning to understand the reasons for their success. Consider these specific companies:

- Xilinx, a $2.4 billion global semiconductor design company, used social media to link its five hundred design engineers with the customers for whom they design custom chips. The result: a 25 percent bump in productivity, higher quality designs, and increased customer satisfaction.[2]

- FICO, an analytics company that created the industry-standard FICO® credit score, was allowed by government regulations to tell consumers their credit scores and the main factors determining those scores, but it could not provide advice about how to improve the scores. To provide that information, they catalyzed a community of customers in their myFICO forums[3] to share techniques among themselves for improving scores.[4]

- CEMEX, the multibillion-dollar global cement and building materials company, directly engaged more than eighteen thousand of its people to make unprecedented progress far faster than expected on the key strategies for creating the company's future.[5]

- When Ford Motor Company introduced SYNC technology they recognized the need for a customer support mechanism that was as sophisticated as the technology itself. So they successfully engaged a community of customers to help each other answer questions on how to use and get the most out of SYNC's capabilities.[6]

- The Schwab Trading Community gets active traders to share information and help each other trade more effectively, with the goal of increasing the wealth of individual participants. Although Schwab doesn't directly target revenue generation with this social-media effort, its new customer engagement creates the opportunity for competitive differentiation.

Schwab has over ten thousand community participants who, on average, complete three hundred and sixty trades per year, versus two hundred trades per year for nonparticipants.[7]

Such solo applications aren't the real story, however. Some of these organizations are now moving beyond one-off efforts and forging a strategic corporate competence around social media. They are transforming themselves into early examples of what we call *social organizations*.

A social organization is one that strategically applies mass collaboration to address significant business challenges and opportunities. Its leaders recognize that becoming a social enterprise is not about incremental improvement. They know it demands a new way of thinking, and so they're moving beyond tactical, one-time grassroots efforts and pushing for greater business impact through a thoughtful, planned approach to applying social media. As a result, a social organization is able to be more agile, produce better outcomes, and even develop entirely new ways of operating that are only achievable through mobilizing the collective talent, energy, ideas, and efforts of communities.

In a social organization, employees, customers, suppliers, and all other stakeholders can participate directly in the creation of value. They contribute to, review, and comment on any phase of the firm's work. In many cases they even participate directly in delivering business value. They're all integral parts of how the firm does its work, and they work together to get the greatest value from the company's products and services.

We see firms, like those noted above, that are amplifying their capabilities through mass collaboration. They've turned employees and customers into effective sales and marketing forces, converted customers into customer support teams, productively made prospects members of their product design teams, and turned vast groups of engineers into innovation engines.

Look at CEMEX, which is using social media as a key element of its strategic global initiative to change fundamentally how the company works and collaborates. In the late 2000s, CEMEX embarked on transformational change to deal with the aftermath of the global financial crisis. Executives considered using the same top-down approach that had worked so well a few years earlier, but they quickly realized the company and its challenges had changed dramatically. Revenues had grown—largely through acquisitions—from $4.3 billion in 1999 to $14.5 billion in 2009—and CEMEX had become one of the world's largest building materials companies, with more than forty-seven thousand employees in one hundred countries.

"More than half of the executives joined the company in the last few years as the result of mergers and acquisitions," says innovation director Miguel Lozano. "And because of growth in emerging markets, we are getting younger—roughly 30 percent of our employees are Gen X."[8]

Thus, while acquisitions had fragmented the company, its strategic goals required a coordinated global response, one CEMEX could not wait to develop and deploy country by country. "We needed to connect ideas, people, and talent in new ways and create a different culture," says Gilberto Garcia, head of innovation.[9] Given these circumstances, executives realized that transformation executed from the top would be slow, expensive, and uneven, and they faced challenges that required speed, flexibility, and global impact.

Consequently, CEMEX initiated a program called SHIFT that used social media to create a community around each of the company's strategic initiatives:

- Sustainability

- New market strategies and channels

- Fuel and energy efficiency

- Creating a twenty-first-century company

- Global transformation of collaboration practices

In total, SHIFT engaged eighteen thousand active users. Each initiative used social media to create an online, worldwide community open to any employee. Two executives, one focused on the business and the other on technical issues, supported each community, which was responsible for defining its initiative in detail, identifying and implementing operational improvements, creating a long-range plan, and putting that plan into practice. A central innovation team supported SHIFT, was responsible for the collaborative environment, provided coaching support to the communities, and facilitated its governance processes.

SHIFT was designed to engage the entire company in discussion, debate, and action around the company's strategic initiatives. As Lozano explained, "Operationally, we work as individual countries and regions or markets. The challenge is to get everyone involved regardless of location, job, or language. SHIFT enables us to develop initiatives at incredible speed by taking the structure of the company—and a person's place in the organization—out of the discussion, so that we can all work together and move faster. SHIFT creates a truly global organization." Based on the success he'd seen, he said, "With SHIFT, I know that we can mobilize the company faster and more effectively."[10]

What we can begin to see at CEMEX and a few other companies is the full promise of social media and the mass collaboration it enables. In these organizations, mass collaboration is beginning to deliver some of the benefits and features of collaborative start-ups we noted at the beginning.

These pioneering social organizations don't simply succeed here and there in using social technology. Instead, they embed mass collaboration in who they are and how they work. It's part of the way they do business; it's how they think. They develop the complex corporate skills to use it well. Thus, they're able to use it again and again to deliver real business value, both inside and outside the enterprise, all along their value chain. They are consistently bringing to bear on problems and opportunities a far greater chunk of people's talents, experience, innovation, and passion than traditional organizations are able to do.

Whether you're the CEO or a manager somewhere along your firm's value chain, our goal in this book is to provide the insight and knowledge you need to move your firm along the path to becoming a social organization. We begin by describing the engine of this social revolution, mass collaboration itself: its key components, its defining characteristics, how it works, and how it's being used. Then we outline an approach to developing the capabilities of a social organization and explore in depth each of the key steps in that evolution. This is the bulk of the book—a description of what your company must do to make progress down the road to becoming a social organization. Finally, we help you assess where your organization currently stands and what it must do next.

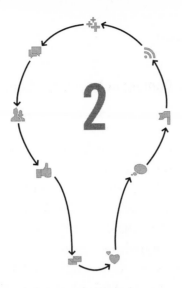

Mass Collaboration
The Heart of the Matter

NOW THAT WE'VE OUTLINED the promise of social media and the advantages of becoming a social organization, we can talk more specifically about how to go about achieving that goal.

First and foremost, what's important here is not social media but what it allows. Social media is a means to an end, not the end itself. Social media enables *mass collaboration*, in which a large and diverse group of people who may have no preexisting connections pursues a mutual purpose that creates value. We call a group of people engaged in mass collaboration a *collaborative community*. It is through communities built around mass collaboration that a social organization is able to enlist the interests, knowledge, talent, and experience of everyone along its value chain to create results that exceed those possible using traditional processes and small-group collaboration.

Three Key Components of Mass Collaboration

What exactly is mass collaboration?

Most people know how to make themselves productive. Managers say they understand how to make teams productive. But how do you make whole communities productive? How do you unearth, define, grow, mobilize, solve problems with, and derive business value from a community as a whole? Simply providing social media isn't enough. A main ingredient—*purpose*—is crucial. Social media, community, and purpose are the indispensable components that together produce mass collaboration (see figure 2-1).[1]

Social Media

Social media is an online environment created for the purpose of mass collaboration. It is where mass collaboration occurs, not the technology per se. For example, Facebook is a social media environment built on social networking technology, and Wikipedia is a social media environment built on wiki technology.

The technology must have a purpose, an end-use, for it to become social media. Without a specific aim (like the Wikipedia

FIGURE 2-1

Components of mass collaboration

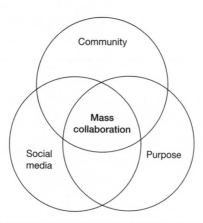

Encyclopedia), it's just technology. Though you can do many things with social media, such as one-to-one interactions and mass communications, its real and unique value comes from mass collaboration—not just any collaboration, but *mass* collaboration.

Social media is powered by a new set of mass collaboration–enabling technologies. These technologies comprise an array of group communication, authoring, and organizational tools that make it possible for large groups of people to collaborate—including such technologies as wikis, blogs, microblogs, social networking, social bookmarking, tagging and tag clouds, social feedback, discussion forums, idea engines, answer marketplaces, prediction markets, and virtual worlds.

Tools to support collaboration have existed for decades. But social media technologies, such as the ones just listed, enable collaboration on a much grander scale. They allow hundreds, thousands, even millions of people to simultaneously create content, share experiences, build relationships, and do other forms of productive work.

Community

Communities are collections of individuals who come together to pursue a common purpose. Bound by their shared purpose, a community can bring a diverse group of people together from inside and outside an organization as well from all levels within the organization.

The ability of large numbers of individuals to form a community around a purpose and to contribute seamlessly, efficiently, and effectively to the collective effort is what makes social media–enabled mass collaboration unique. Without a community, there is no mass collaboration.

Purpose

Purpose is what draws people together into a community. It is the cause around which people rally, the link that turns individuals into members of a community. It defines a community. It is what leads members to contribute their knowledge, experience, and ideas.

Purpose is the measuring stick for assessing the effectiveness of the community, the suitability of the social technologies selected, the value of business objectives, and the effectiveness of management guidance.

In fact, purpose serves a dual function. A strong purpose attracts people to create and contribute to a community. It provides personal value. It also provides value to the business, and that value is what motivates firms to adopt social media and join or sponsor collaborative communities.

"But," we often hear, "communities on the public Internet seem to appear and grow spontaneously to millions of participants without an obvious, explicit purpose." That may be the appearance, but almost all successful social Web sites started with a defined purpose and limited scope. Facebook started at Harvard as a way for students and graduates to keep in touch.[2] Craigslist was launched in San Francisco as a place where software engineers could share information on local events of interest.[3] MySpace participation took off only after the site targeted music bands and clubs in Los Angeles and grew from there.[4] In fact, other popular websites have never much expanded beyond their original purpose. YouTube still focuses mostly on letting users upload and share personal videos. And Wikipedia continues to focus on building an online encyclopedia.

Think of the three components this way: Community is the people *who* collaborate. Social media is *where* they collaborate. And purpose is *why* they collaborate. Social media plus community plus purpose create mass collaboration. And extensive, repeated success with mass collaboration in collaborative communities characterizes a social organization. Simple. But, like much else in organizations, this simple idea can be hard to execute well.

Six Principles of Mass Collaboration

The city manager of a small Texas city ardently opposed the use of social media. He put an e-mail address on the city's website and asked residents to contribute ideas for improving city services. Not only was the flood of responses more than his staff could handle, but most came from people living not only outside his city but outside Texas. His conclusion: "Social media is an unmanageable waste of resources." His experience was indeed a bad one. But like other efforts we see in many organizations, what he did wasn't social media and it certainly wasn't mass collaboration.

Mass collaboration is defined by six fundamental principles or defining characteristics.[5] Participation, collective, transparency, independence, persistence, and emergence, in combination, set it apart from other forms of communication and collaboration. A social media implementation that doesn't display all these principles won't enable mass collaboration.

- *Participation:* To achieve substantial benefits from social media, you must mobilize a community to contribute. It's often said that "the user is the application," which means that all value in social media comes from user participation. In most effective social media environments, the vast majority of content comes from community participants. That means you can't capture the wisdom of crowds if crowds don't participate. Many organizations overlook this principle and consider social media just another channel for broadcasting corporate communications. Imagine Wikipedia, YouTube, Craigslist, Facebook, MySpace, LinkedIn, or any other marquee social site without user-generated content. They would all be empty shells.

- *Collective:* In a collaborative community, participants "collect" voluntarily around a unifying purpose. People collect in Facebook to stay connected with those they know and to make new connections. People collect on Wikipedia to create encyclopedia articles. People collect on YouTube to share videos. In these examples, and in all social media, participants contribute to the whole rather than create content and distribute it individually—via, say, e-mail. This act of contributing to the collective effort, which is constantly being created and expanded through a multitude of independent contributions, is what's new with mass collaboration. The collective principle distinguishes mass collaboration approaches from such distribution-based approaches and technologies as e-mail, file transfer, and broadcast media.

- *Transparency:* To create mass collaboration, a social media solution must provide transparency, which means all participants see each other's contributions. They get to see, use, reuse, augment, validate, critique, and rate what everyone adds to the collective. Without transparency, there can be no participant collaboration on content. Executed properly, transparency gives a community the information needed to self-organize members' contributions and create meaning out of what could easily become an unusable quagmire of content. Because of transparency, the community is able to apply content more intelligently, improve content, unify information, self-govern, self-correct, and evolve—from which community consensus, decisions, and other results can emerge. Seeing others' contributions is often what attracts participants and inspires them to contribute. Transparency distinguishes mass collaboration from other forms of content sharing such as surveys, shared directories, search engines, Web content management, and traditional knowledge management. And, far from least, transparency breeds trust, which fosters even more participation. The Texas city implementation completely missed the transparency principle. People were unable to view, comment on, and validate each other's contributions. As a result, their mass collaboration turned into unmanageable "mess" collaboration.

- *Independence:* Independence delivers *anytime, anyplace, any member* collaboration, which means any participant can contribute completely independent of any other. Participants can collaborate no matter where they are or whoever else may be posting content at that time; no coordination of collaboration or preexisting relationships is required. Participation is not predetermined by an e-mail list or any other explicit relationship mechanism. There is no workflow mechanism or document check-in/check-out process that can bottleneck or limit the scale of collaboration. For example, wiki technology has taken off primarily because of its inline editing capability that allows anytime, anyplace, anyone updates.

- *Persistence:* Participant contributions are captured and kept for others to view, share, and augment. Such persistence distinguishes mass collaboration from, say, synchronous conversations where much of the information exchanged is either lost or only partially preserved. Organizations that use social media–enabled mass collaboration must determine how much persistence they want. Understanding what information should persist, how long it should be held, and how to capture it in the least burdensome manner are significant design concerns for social media solutions.

- *Emergence:* The behaviors in mass collaboration cannot be modeled, designed, optimized, or controlled like traditional systems. They simply emerge over time through the interactions of community members. Emergence is what allows collaborative communities to come up with new ways of working or new solutions to seemingly intractable problems; it is the source of innovation as good ideas appear and rise in prominence through collaboration. What emerges will vary with each community and its purpose and may include latent or hidden relationships, expertise, new work processes, new ways to organize content, and much more. From contributions to Wikipedia, for example, is emerging a rich network of interrelated information created when contributors link their content to the content of others within and outside Wikipedia.

A social organization is highly skilled at applying all these core principles to ensure that communities actually practice mass collaboration. We can see them at work in the way collaborative communities function.

How a Collaborative Community Works

How can a thousand, ten thousand, or a million people do actual work and produce something meaningful to them and useful to an organization? Why doesn't that number of people just produce chaos? You would think an organization of a thousand people, even if they're located in one place, needs division of labor, hierarchy, and management to be productive. Above all, of course, a collaborative community needs a common purpose, as well as the six principles or characteristics of mass collaboration we just described. But, even then, how does anything useful actually get done?

Behind the vast and expanding array of social technologies and applications now available sits a metacycle of activity more or less common to all mass collaboration. It consists of four basic actions or stages: contributions, feedback, judgment, and change, as shown in figure 2-2.

- *Contributions:* The whole process starts with community members' contributions—thoughts, ideas, opinions, suggestions, and even questions or problems. Contributions are the foundation—the raw material—for all else.

- *Feedback:* Once members contribute, other members provide feedback; they visit, rate, comment on, and otherwise express their take on the value of the contribution, thus enhancing it with the collective opinion of the community. In many communities, the value of contributions is directly rated by community members. It's also possible for members to flag content as inappropriate (abusive, personal attack, and so on, based on the standards of the community).

- *Judgment:* Through multisided discussion and various means of feedback aggregation, contributions are judged and assessed by the community. This validation builds the status and reputation of both contributions and contributors. Good contributions and contributors can gain points, literal or figurative, that elevate their status and visibility. In short,

FIGURE 2-2

The fundamental cycle of collaboration

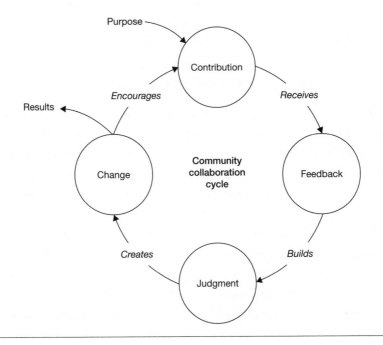

through feedback that's aggregated into some sort of judgment, the community separates the worthwhile from the worthless, the useful from the useless. Through a collective evaluation process, contributions considered most valuable by the community will float to the surface.

If a community has no transparent means to judge through voting, leader boards, or some other device, there will be no mass collaboration—just a giant unmanageable suggestion box. Organizations often leave this piece out and then complain, "All we got was a flood of ideas and opinions that we couldn't possibly go through and use."

- *Change:* Transparent feedback and evaluation nudges participation in desirable directions as members see what contributions and behaviors are considered valuable or not. Members think, "How do I get on the leader board?" or "I don't want to be 'badged' aggressive. How do I avoid that?" If this is all done well, members will emulate the good, avoid the bad, and evolve community and organizational productivity to higher levels for better results. These new behaviors and changes then influence members' behavior in general, as well as subsequent contributions, and the cycle repeats.

These steps are how communities self-learn, self-govern, and self-direct. In many social media failures, we see conditions that prevent this cycle from functioning properly. A social organization, on the other hand, knows how to promote the cycle and guard its health. When it's working well, the cycle is the foundation for a thriving, productive, and self-sustaining community.

In active communities, the continuous flow of content kicks off numerous, simultaneous, and often very rapid iterations of this cycle. We've made the cycle look neat when, in fact, it will most often seem chaotic in practice, especially in the early stages of a community's life. The magic of technology-enabled mass collaboration is that from this apparent chaos can emerge productive outcomes through the kind of aggregated judgment we've just described.

To see how this works, look at CEMEX and the community it created to directly engage over five hundred of its people across the world around one of its strategic initiatives—increased use of alternative fuels in its plants. This was its purpose, its cause. It made progress by passing through the cycle several times.[6]

- *First iteration of the cycle:* Early contributions and feedback quickly focused on the question, "What's the first thing we should do?" From the varied responses, one answer emerged: Survey all the plants to find those that are currently best at using alternative fuels and see what can be learned from them.

- *Second iteration:* This was straightforward—all the plants contributed data about their use of fuels. Questions were asked, and issues raised and addressed. Within a couple of weeks, community feedback identified the most efficient plants.

- *Third iteration:* The managers of the best plants ran webcasts explaining to the community what they did and how they did it. The community posted questions, comments, and feedback: "We tried it, and it worked well" or "We tried your approach, but here are the results we got." Through that feedback and discussion, the best plants' procedures were improved even more and best practices emerged that recognized differences between plants. As they understood the practices, plant engineers began changing how they operated their own plants until the best practices had been adopted around the world with the result of increasing CEMEX's use of alternative fuels.

What if CEMEX management had taken the more traditional approach of (1) assembling a team to go out and audit all plants to identify the practices of the best ones and then (2) directing other plants to adopt those practices? It would have taken much longer, achieved a lower-quality assessment, and faced huge adoption challenges. Most likely, dozens of plants would have dragged their feet or claimed, "We can't do that here." In the end, management said the engineers had accomplished in six weeks using mass collaboration what would normally have taken two years.

New Ways for the Masses to Collaborate

Based on the four-stage cycle, collaborative communities can perform a variety of disparate tasks, such as generating innovative ideas, solving difficult challenges, engineering and improving product, fostering product usage, building brand awareness, gaining better market insight, creating corporate memory, managing complex documentation, and on and on. In fact, we are seeing the following patterns emerge—ways that communities mass collaborate to achieve bigger, faster, and better results.[7]

Collective Intelligence

Collective intelligence is the pooling of small and incremental community contributions into a coherent, useful body of knowledge. Participants post content, augment it, categorize it, rate it, and link it to other content. Blogs, wikis, media sharing, and discussion forums are the most prevalent social media technologies supporting collective intelligence. For example, a skyscraper window cleaning company felt its business was too dependent on a few foremen who knew how to rig sophisticated scaffolding. It fostered a community of foremen who worked together to create a multimedia knowledge base of rigging techniques.

Expertise Location

Expertise location is about finding the right expert, solution, idea, innovation, passionate customer, and so on in a large community. It focuses on *selective* intelligence, as opposed to collective intelligence, and the goal is not to collect and amalgamate small contributions from the masses but to find in the masses exactly the knowledge or resource needed. *Crowdsourcing*, a social media phenomenon, is a form of expertise location.

A good example is the consumer electronics company that discovered a handful of customers (out of millions) who were both passionate and highly knowledgeable about the company's products and were willing to answer other customers' questions. A company executive said that the only people more knowledgeable about their products were product engineers—and product engineers weren't staffing the call center. By using these customers, the company drastically improved time-to-issue-resolution while significantly driving down support costs.

Emergent Structures

Emergent structures are processes, content-categorization schemes, organizational networks, hidden virtual teams, and the like that are unknown or unplanned before social interactions but emerge through the four-phase collaboration cycle. The goal of looking for or pursuing emergent structures is a better understanding of "how things work"—how organizations actually, informally behave and accomplish goals. Community members don't explicitly contribute this information, of course. It emerges, often through use of specific social technologies as noted above—social network analysis, idea engines, answer marketplaces, prediction markets, social tagging, social bookmarking, and social analytics. For example, using social network analysis, a global manufacturing company analyzed the work of over four hundred R&D employees in thirty-eight countries to identify those working on similar projects and facilitate their collaboration.[8]

Interest Cultivation

Interest cultivation is aimed at collecting people and content around a common interest with the goal of growing the community and increasing their level of engagement. Participants post information about what they like and others rate their likes and add their opinions. Highly rated and active "likes" gain prominence and become easy for others to discover. Organizations pursuing interest cultivation employ blogs, discussion forums, social publishing, and social feedback as key social media technologies.

Barnes & Noble is a great example of interest cultivation. It takes a multi-channel approach to social media, using its barnesandnoble.com forums, Facebook, Twitter, and blogs to cultivate communities around a shared passion for reading. The B&N Community on barnesandnoble.com has about 5 million visitors and twenty thousand posts per month.[9] Their B&N and Nook pages on Facebook also enjoy substantial activity. For example, the B&N Facebook page has more than six hundred and seventy thousand likes (fans who say they like the pages) and almost six hundred discussion topics, with numerous posts within topics.[10] Barnes & Noble is experiencing 30 to 50 percent organic growth in the Facebook fan base per quarter. People gravitate to the communities to discuss books and genres; post questions, answers, and recommendations; and help each other "find their next great read." Community members and fans are engaged with each other and the company—and tend to be more loyal customers who are projected to generate higher lifetime value.

Mass Coordination for Rapid Response

Mass coordination involves rapidly organizing a large community of people through fast and short mass messaging, often spread virally. Participants send short messages to groups of "followers" and quickly rally people around a happening or an event. The best-known form of mass coordination is *flash mobbing*. A good example was the Facebook-facilitated "flashdance" at the Liverpool train station where thousands of dancers filled the station and simultaneously began dancing. Another example: in 2010 there was a significant backlash by mothers on Twitter (@motrinmoms) and YouTube against a Motrin ad portraying babies as a fashion accessory that causes back pain.

Organizational use of mass coordination is growing—for example, for rapid response to material outages, staffing shortages, accidents, and inclement weather. A hotel chain uses it to rapidly propagate money-saving best practices across multiple properties.

Relationship Leverage

Relationship leverage is the practice of maintaining and deriving value from a prodigious number of relationships. It is driven primarily by blogging and social networking technologies. Participants express their opinions, hoping they will resonate with others and generate a following. For example, Bill Marriot, CEO of Marriot Hotels and Resorts, uses a blog to build weak-tie relationships with potentially millions of people who feel connected with him because they know what he thinks about a number of issues. Because he need only respond to relatively few blog comments, he is able to maintain a huge number of relationships with little effort.[11]

Mass Collaboration and the Social Organization

An organization becomes a social organization when it discovers the power of mass collaboration and develops the necessary corporate skills to address challenges by readily and repeatedly creating collaborative communities.

To do this requires a new and different mind-set. The people in a social organization no longer think entirely in terms of hierarchy and traditional management. They don't automatically respond to a challenge by assigning its resolution to some person or group or by creating a structured process to deal with it. Because they've integrated community collaboration into the way they work and think every day, they ask instead: "Can a community do it better? Can we form a community to deal more effectively with this?" If the answer is yes, it takes that approach.

Consequently, the way a social organization manages, the way it invests, the way its systems work, and the way its people think are all different from the way organizations have traditionally worked.

The benefits are real and increasingly obvious. Mobilizing collaborative communities can help you sense and react more rapidly to changes in the operating environment, assess more quickly what's working and what isn't, and determine how to respond and influence outcomes. Involving the community not only provides better intelligence and decisions, but it also fosters more rapid adoption of change since the community already feels involved and vested in the effort.

By consistently and effectively mobilizing communities, a social organization can gain a competitive edge in just about any aspect of their business that involves people. For example, involving the people who will use a product, service, or process in its design will produce a superior outcome by increasing the chances of meeting users' needs. At every stage of the value chain, people are more likely to use and derive value from something they had a hand in creating. A social organization recognizes that this act of listening and encouraging participation not only produces better results, it also forges closer ongoing relationships and creates a more efficient operating model. It's an approach in which everyone wins.

In short, the ability to tap productively into the full knowledge, talent, innovation, and energy of large groups of people—something never before possible—can make the social organization quicker, more innovative, more nimble, more responsive to the marketplace, and more focused. In short, it can lift an enterprise to a new level of capability.

It's Not Easy

But be warned. "We are a social organization" is not something a company can simply declare or assert. Becoming a social organization requires a strategic approach, deliberate choice, and steadfast intention as the organization proceeds through an evolution of thinking and skills based on actually using collaborative communities and achieving tangible benefits. Not least, it also requires thoughtful management guidance both to keep communities focused on valued and valuable purposes and to keep communities linked productively to the organization as a whole.

Choosing community collaboration over traditional approaches will challenge the organization and individual managers within it. Companies that prefer to operate via prescribed processes, are obsessed with defining roles and responsibilities in great detail, and place great store in formal hierarchy will struggle to become social organizations. Managers who consider formal authority the primary tool at their disposal for influencing others will wrestle individually with their roles and functions in managing a community. And all managers will need to reconcile the tension between their continuing responsibility for outcomes with their inability to mandate or control what a collaborative community will produce.

In spite of these challenges, though, companies are increasingly using collaborative communities, finding real benefits, and concluding, in the words of Miguel Lozano, Innovation Director at CEMEX: "Now that we've done it this way . . . we'll never go back to the old way."[12]

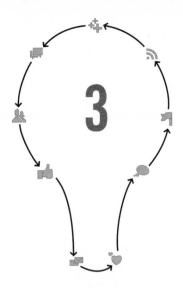

Becoming a Social Organization

A consumer goods company sees the hype and buzz of social media and feels compelled to get involved. So it jumps in and redirects millions of its traditional advertising dollars to a social media effort in hopes of selling more product. A large community forms and basically interacts as the company intended. Yet the company doesn't sell more product. The promotion over, it lets the community dissipate.

Meanwhile, the company knows its distributors are using social media because it hears of successes here and failures there, but it's uncomfortable because it really doesn't know what's going on. So it puts in place a restrictive social networking policy. But the sales force pushes back and says it needs flexibility with the social Web in order to sell effectively. PR and Marketing also resist, and so the company creates a second policy, and then a third. A disgruntled employee tweets that his boss is a jerk and that he is fed up with the company leadership's abusive culture. That little message gets retweeted 672,324 times. The company fires the employee, who sues for wrongful termination, claiming freedom of speech, conflicting policy, and that Twitter is a microblog, not a social network.

While all that's going on, the IT department, wanting in on social media, replaces the corporate directory with a social network. Adoption is dismal because, it turns out, no one uses the corporate directory and neither knows nor cares that it was replaced. So IT tries again and puts a wiki in place to see what happens. People actually start using it, put in more and more requests for additional functionality, and start calling with technical questions and problems. IT didn't count on this burden, and now it needs more resources or it will suffer yet another blow to its reputation.

Then HR informs the CEO that a large community of employees has formed on the wiki, protesting the new health-care plans and demanding that HR change them. The CEO was already concerned about relations between employees and management. This information comes just one day after the competitive intelligence team briefed the executive team about the press the company's chief competitor is getting for its leading-edge social media efforts.

Sound familiar? This story—a social media nightmare filled with HR problems, missed opportunities, quiet failures, possible threats, and hidden successes—is hyperbole, but a less dramatic version of it is happening today in many, if not most, medium-sized and large firms. Indeed, all these things have happened in real companies. These challenges stem from a single root cause: the companies had no thoughtful approach to social media and community collaboration, so they are limited to reactive measures as things pop up.

Unfortunately, in circumstances like these, most companies respond with policy rather than strategy. Without a thoughtful approach, their social media problems will only get worse.

Contrary to the claims of some early advocates, social media efforts rarely produce good outcomes spontaneously. As we noted in chapter 1, this was the first and most obvious insight we gained from our study of over four hundred companies. Most organizations we've seen simply provide access to social media technology and hope that the magic of collaboration just happens—a practice we call *provide-and-pray*.

Our research indicates that only around 10 percent of such provide-and-pray initiatives succeed. The vast majority (about 70 percent) fall short because adoption is insignificant and no active community emerges. The remaining 20 percent fail because, though a community does form, it never delivers genuine value to the organization.

From all the cases we've studied, we can identify a few common reasons for failure:

- Social media initiatives fail most frequently because organizations focus on the technologies when they should focus instead on achieving a purpose through the new collective behaviors that those technologies make possible. New behaviors aimed at purpose, not technology, provide business value. Social media technology is a crucial component, but it's an enabler with little or no value by itself. Its worth arises from what it allows.

- They fail because the organization lacks knowledge of the fundamental principles of mass collaboration. Not even great technology will save those efforts that ignore or omit the basic characteristics of successful social initiatives.

- They fail because not all challenges are well suited to mass collaboration. Organizations need to understand where collective communities are most likely to provide real value. Using mass collaboration in settings where it's not appropriate wastes people's time and the firm's money and can even expose organizations to the possibility of mismanaging important information.

- Finally, they fail because the organization's executives and managers lack the confidence to assign compelling purposes to communities and then allow the communities to find a way to fulfill their purposes. Managers stifle innovation with interference and excessive oversight, and, when the community does innovate, they lack ways to turn those ideas into organizational change.

When organizations merely make social media available and then nothing meaningful happens, they blame the tools, conclude that social media lacks business value, or assume their organizations simply aren't ready. More often than not, however, the truth is more basic: they didn't do it right. They didn't take it seriously. They didn't invest or prepare properly. They treated social media like some collaboration panacea driven by technology so naturally attractive it could succeed on its own.

That's the bad news: social media succeeds by itself only once in a blue moon. But there's good news as well: there are mass collaboration practices and techniques we've seen used successfully in many organizations of all sizes, industries, and cultures.

An Approach That Enables Repeatable Success

In this book we offer a multistep approach that gathers those practices and techniques into a coherent whole (see figure 3-1). This approach won't guarantee success, but it will significantly increase the odds in your favor. It's based on practices common among successful efforts that, taken together, constitute a way an enterprise can use mass collaboration strategically to become a social organization.

We know the idea of a prescribed approach doesn't sit well with many social media advocates. It implies management, and they consider management anathema to the heart and spirit of mass collaboration. In their world management means stifling controls and narrow limits on creativity and spontaneity. Management is the cold hand that grips most organizations and chills the human spirit.

Of course, these advocates are the same people who advise companies to provide the technology and watch as communities mysteriously form and create brilliant solutions to intractable problems. It would be nice if the world worked that way, and if you and your company can tolerate the kind of 1-in-10 ratio that spells success in venture capital, where one megahit compensates for a stream of failures, you might consider provide-and-pray. But, if that's not the world you work in, consider the approach presented here.

FIGURE 3-1

The process for becoming a social organization

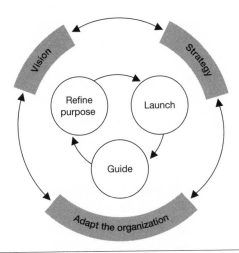

We hasten to add that there's management and there's management. Using a defined approach to manage social media *can* stifle innovation and creativity. It *can* make social media into just another means of command and control. It *can* make a mockery of collaboration. But done right, management can create an organizational culture and context where community collaboration thrives. The trick, of course, is to manage social media in a way that avoids the bad and fosters the good.

In spite of the dangers, there are compelling reasons to use a defined approach. It can:

- *Increase the likelihood of success* when you create collaborative communities. Like checklists used by pilots before takeoff, a defined approach can make sure you're doing all the essentials. In particular, it can increase the chances that collaborative communities will produce results that help the organization achieve its mission and goals.

- *Enhance the business impact of success* because it focuses community collaboration on important business challenges and opportunities rather than ad hoc and random communities.

- *Provide important transparency* for all involved, if done right. They know who's doing what, and why, and they understand their own roles.

- *Help you move from a few one-off successes to a repeatable competence* that produces repeated successes. Repeatable success will lift your enterprise to a new level of capability and make it a social organization that learns and improves continuously. Without a defined approach, there is no way to understand what worked and build on success while minimizing challenges.

- *Ensure that the right people are involved.* Social media must be a business-led effort. Though it will be technology enabled—and so IT certainly should be involved—IT should be a participant, not the leader, especially in the early stages of the effort. Focusing on technology too early would be a fundamental and even catastrophic error. Social media must be seen as a business capability, not an IT project.

The approach we suggest is a flexible framework—a guide to action, not a series of highly specific steps that must be carried out exactly as described and in the order given. Indeed, some of the activities we outline can be done concurrently when that makes sense. Some steps in some situations should be repeated; thus the approach will iterate. And all of it should be adapted—thoughtfully, carefully—to the particulars of your organization and your goals for community collaboration.

Building competence of any kind requires practice—starting with small steps and building success on success. This is critical in mass collaboration because the necessary trust, along with the willingness to share and work together, require time and practice to build and take hold. A defined approach can thus act as a learning cycle—*do, review, learn, do again*—that an organization repeats continually to build the competence and confidence to take on larger challenges.

The goal of the approach is to build your organization's capability for repeatable success with mass collaboration. In the summary below and in the remainder of the book we will progress through the main activities of the approach, as depicted in figure 3-1: vision, strategy, refine purpose, launch, guide, and adapt the organization.

Develop an Organizational Vision for Community Collaboration

To make mass collaboration an organizational capability, leaders must begin by developing an enterprise-wide vision of where community collaboration can create value for the organization. Developing such a vision comprises four activities:

- *Understand when community collaboration is appropriate:* Communities are not the answer for all collaboration challenges. Organizations can expose themselves to significant risk if they apply mass collaboration inappropriately. In developing a vision, organizations must clearly understand the kinds of problems and opportunities where community collaboration can add value.

- *Know where community collaboration is more likely to deliver value:* When creating a vision for community collaboration, start with some knowledge of where it has already succeeded (see the discussion in chapter 2 of common reasons companies currently use it). This will provide insight into areas of lesser and greater risk. You should know if you're exploring new territory or if many have passed before you. Also, an idea of what's going on with other industries can shed light on areas of competitive advantage and competitive necessity.

- *Apply an understanding of your organization's goals and culture:* A social organization can repeatedly apply community collaboration as a basic corporate competence to address important business challenges and opportunities. To achieve this level of capability, examine your organizational goals and explicitly link them to your community collaboration efforts. It's also important, right from the start, to understand the culture of your organization and, in particular, current attitudes toward social media. You will need to accommodate them as you proceed.

- *Finally, craft an organizational vision for community collaboration:* To craft an organizational vision, you need to develop *community collaboration opportunity statements* that identify specific areas where community collaboration can support the success of your organization. These statements are the heart of the vision, since they give people a tangible sense of how community collaboration can change the way the organization pursues its goals. They also provide a glimpse into a possible future in which the company operates more like a social organization.

At the end of the vision stage of the process, you will have a document with two related parts: the first will consist of a declaration in which leadership explicitly recognizes the potential of community collaboration; the second will consist of a set of statements identifying areas of opportunity where mass collaboration can help the organization reach its goals. As a whole, the vision paints a partial but vivid picture of a future where community collaboration is the norm.

Develop an Organizational Strategy for Community Collaboration

Be prepared, when you publish the vision, because it may unleash a flood of requests for additional collaborative communities. This can be paralyzing—or an opportunity for transformation. It will depend on whether your organization can quickly, systematically, and prudently decide which community collaboration efforts to pursue, where and how to invest resources in them, and how to begin the journey to becoming a social organization in a way that won't overwhelm the company. This is the role of *strategy*.

Organizational strategy for community collaboration comprises continuous planning that identifies where you will apply mass collaboration to foster collaborative communities that create real business value. Building the strategy is done in three main activities:

- Establishing how to intelligently select, from the multitude of community collaboration possibilities, those that the organization should pursue

- Determining where and when to invest, or continue investing, in specific collaborative communities

- Building a business justification for select collaborative communities

These activities happen at the level of the whole organization, in order to manage investment holistically in a portfolio of collaborative communities.

Cultivate Collaborative Communities

Now the process moves to the actual cultivation of *individual* communities and the three iterative steps required to refine purpose, launch, and guide them (see figure 3-2).

Refine Purpose by Creating a Purpose Roadmap

A purpose is the reason people collaborate, the cause around which they rally. It motivates community members to interact and contribute. But while a community may begin with a single overall purpose, that single purpose will not be enough. Communities will tackle many purposes over time. Evolving purposes fuel communities and keep them vibrant. If that fuel runs out, a community will stop. This is what purpose roadmaps are for. A *purpose roadmap* is a set of related purposes that flow into the future from the original purpose, are aligned over time, and identify options for how the community can evolve. The roadmap serves as a guide for the development, growth, and maintenance of the community. In chapter 6 we describe how to build a purpose roadmap, which will

FIGURE 3-2

Creating and sustaining a collaborative community requires three iterative steps

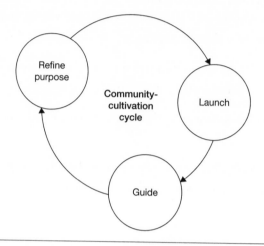

provide the critical planning and justification information needed to proceed to launch.

Launch the Community

Launch takes the community from opportunity and purpose to reality and includes a variety of activities, most notably:

- *Define the community collaboration experience:* Describe explicitly how community members should interact with one another and how the environment will provide an easy, useful, and meaningful member experience. Explore what will motivate members to engage deeply and often. From this, understand and define the participant behaviors you want.

- *Plan community engagement:* You will need a *tipping-point plan* that describes how to gain attention, draw in participation, and move the community to the tipping point—the critical mass of participation at which a community achieves viral growth and becomes self-sustaining. Successful communities do not grow slowly over time, they reach the tipping point quickly.

- *Deliver the community collaboration environment:* Here you will focus on the development of the social media environment itself, its features and capabilities, how it works, and, above all, the user experience it offers. This also includes deciding if and how to participate in an existing environment as an alternative to creating something new.

At the completion of this stage, you will have done all you can to foster the creation of a successful collaborative community.

Guide the Community

This is where the collaborative community forms and does its work. This is where it creates value for itself and the organization. And this is where traditional management can compromise the principles of mass collaboration. In a social organization, management guides mass collaboration, rather than directing or controlling it.

The term *guide* refers to the role of those managers who sponsor a community and are responsible for its results. In a real sense, the preparation that preceded this step was largely about "planning to let go." Once the initiative has been launched and a community forms, it will take on a life of its own and, in large part, become the master of its own destiny. At this point, control will shift from the organization to the community and those in charge until now will move to a role of guiding rather than directing or controlling. Think of it as "managing by guiding from the middle." It's a difficult shift for some managers to make.

Guiding is an ongoing process, and its key aim is to keep a community functioning well and focused on a productive purpose. The challenge here for managers is to apply good principles of leadership and resist the urge to reduce uncertainty with micromanagement, which will strangle a community.

Adapt the Organizational Context

Collaborative communities cannot thrive and reach their potential in a vacuum. Hence, while *guiding* focuses on a community's internal workings, managers must also ensure that the wider organization, the context within which communities operate, supports mass collaboration.

The problem is that the fit between formal organizations and collaborative communities can sometimes be uneasy. For some sense of the difference between the two, recall the discussion in chapter 1 where we contrasted the open, collaborative nature of a start-up with the more formal structure that typically comes with increasing size. Imagine trying to combine the two and you'll have some sense of the tensions that can exist between a free-form collaborative community and a carefully defined, prescriptive hierarchy.

It is the job of management to mediate this relationship, and it does so in two key ways:

- *Managers provide the daily, ongoing connection between each community and the formal organization:* To succeed by achieving their purposes, collaborative communities need organizational resources—human, financial, and other— along with the attention of management and access to corporate systems and processes. These needs are unlikely to be met spontaneously. Someone—managers—must create the connective tissue that binds the pieces into a whole. Communities that exist in isolation are *social islands*, relatively small collaborative groups isolated from the rest of the organization. Such islands may be successful within themselves, but they deliver far less value than they could if they were closely connected with the enterprise. Without these connections, the results and recommendations they generate will remain local and limited in value.

- *Managers must also foster organizational changes that facilitate the work of collaborative communities:* Sometimes what is needed goes beyond the day-to-day connections we just discussed. Creating a supportive context for collaboration may call for more fundamental changes in the way corporate leadership, culture, systems, and functions operate. For example, HR may need to adapt the way employees are assessed to include the value of individual contributions made to a community, or Finance may need to adapt its guidelines for evaluating project proposals—by definition, communities cannot predict the outcomes of their work. Managers responsible for the success of collaborative communities must identify such changes and press for their adoption.

Most efforts to create social media–enabled mass collaboration fail to produce anything of value. With this process, you can avoid the major reasons for failure: communities lack a purpose that attracts participation and provides organizational value; executives don't see the value and withhold their support; collaboration is seen only as a technological challenge—another IT project; organizational culture, systems, processes, and policies stifle collaboration; and communities remain social islands that, at best, create value for themselves and not the organization.

The remainder of the book will explore in detail each piece of the process we've outlined here. Using that process to build new levels of corporate competence can lift your firm to the level of a social organization, one that operates at a higher level of capability through mass collaboration.

How Will You Compete?

The multistep approach to becoming a social organization presented in these pages is critical for one final reason. It is how you use mass collaboration to create strategic advantage. You may be tempted to think that, since social media can be used by any organization, it cannot provide competitive differentiation. Don't fall into that trap. Putting mass collaboration to work in your enterprise and becoming a social organization require a high degree of corporate skill that most companies will struggle to develop for many years to come. Some will fall behind when their competitors do become social organizations.

Given that reality, here's what you and every other manager today must ask: What happens when more and more traditional firms crack the code on mass collaboration and begin to demonstrate the superior capabilities of a social organization?

Those organizations that don't incorporate this new capability into the core of how they operate will find it difficult to compete. Why? Because social organizations will be able to get more from people by coalescing them into collaborative communities that innovate and solve their most difficult problems. They are able to have greater impact on the market by creating productive communities of customers and prospects. They are able, in short, to delegate work to communities again and again in a manner that significantly and rapidly expands organizational value.

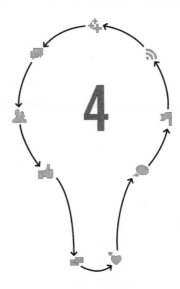

Forming a Vision for Community Collaboration

In 2009–2010, the leaders of NASA's Marshall Space Flight Center (MSFC) knew their manned space program was approaching a decisive moment. Plans for a vehicle to replace the space shuttle had stalled, and the shuttle was nearing its end of life. MSFC's Constellation program and Ares rockets were being heavily criticized by outside scientists and engineers. Public sentiment no longer supported the space program as strongly as it once had. Congress and the president were reexamining the future of the space program and considering significant changes that could diminish NASA's involvement in favor of privatization.

As MSFC leaders began rethinking the nature and value of the space mission, they recognized the importance of involving more people—inside and outside NASA—in the process of dealing with these fundamental questions. And so they began to envision how community collaboration could help them accomplish this mission and increase awareness of the value NASA and MSFC provide to the world.[1] Jonathan Pettus, Chief Information Officer at MSFC, said,

"We believed that social media could have a significant impact on how we pursue our mission. That using it could help us collaborate in new ways to build rockets better. But you can't just put the technology out there and expect big results. It isn't that easy. We are not all the way there yet, but we are moving forward towards our goals, and our focus on vision and purpose has provided a foundation for continued progress."[2] The steps they took will help us understand and explore the important role of a vision for collaboration.

Only recently have organizations begun to employ social media for community collaboration, and they're still learning to use it effectively. Most pursue it sporadically and tactically. But some, like MSFC, are recognizing the power of involving communities more directly and deeply in their mission and operations.

Social organizations broaden their vision of social media and community engagement to address strategic issues. But attitudes toward social media vary greatly and continue to evolve, in many cases from negative to neutral and, ultimately, to positive. Because it's still relatively new for most firms, we advise them to begin with an official vision statement of its potential benefits for the organization.

So, when you prepare your vision statement, open it with an overall expression of belief in the strategic importance of community collaboration, followed by a list of areas in the organization where collaboration can provide substantial benefits. Be specific regarding the areas and how collaboration can be used in each. Pursuing these areas represents the next stage in the evolution of your firm into a highly collaborative social organization. Wrap up your statement with a call to action, and note any sources of additional information or assistance.

A vision statement serves two main purposes. First, it articulates the belief of leadership in the importance and value of community-based collaboration. Second, it concretely identifies significant opportunities for the firm where such collaboration can add value by helping the organization move closer to its goals. Both elements are important. The absence of one will diminish the impact of the other. By itself, a general statement of support for collaboration will be considered little more than empty rhetoric. And merely listing areas where collaboration might help will only elicit the responses, "So what?" and "Says who?" Done well, a vision statement can provide clarity and direction, guide strategy, enhance buy-in, and inspire participation.

To develop an effective vision statement, you need to:

- Understand when community collaboration is appropriate

- Know where community collaboration is more likely to deliver value

- Apply an understanding of your organization's goals and culture

- Craft and distribute an organizational vision for community collaboration

Developing a vision is a creative activity, and brainstorming will play an important role. Like all creative endeavors, it can be somewhat messy, and getting to a valuable, insightful, and inspiring outcome can be a challenge. It will require patience and the involvement of able, knowledgeable people.

Understand When Community Collaboration Is Appropriate

Not all collaboration is appropriate for the masses. Not all challenges lend themselves well to community collaboration. Misuse of social media can expose your organization to high failure rates, mediocre results, and significant information management risks. To avoid these problems, you need to understand when community collaboration is suitable and where it's unlikely to add much value.[3] Figure 4-1 maps out situations where community collaboration is more appropriate and where it's less suitable.

FIGURE 4-1

Suitability of mass collaboration

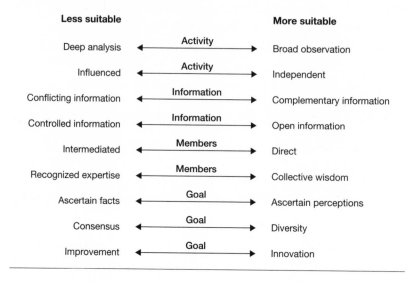

Less suitable		More suitable
Deep analysis	←— Activity —→	Broad observation
Influenced	←— Activity —→	Independent
Conflicting information	←— Information —→	Complementary information
Controlled information	←— Information —→	Open information
Intermediated	←— Members —→	Direct
Recognized expertise	←— Members —→	Collective wisdom
Ascertain facts	←— Goal —→	Ascertain perceptions
Consensus	←— Goal —→	Diversity
Improvement	←— Goal —→	Innovation

Where Community Collaboration Is More Suitable

Community collaboration is more appropriate when large groups of people act independently to contribute and share open and complementary information that aggregates well into a bigger picture and results in actions that lead to heightened performance. The goal in these settings is to accumulate a diversity of information—for example, divergent perspectives, disparate groups' perceptions, and multiple areas of expertise—which is more likely to produce innovative ideas or broader understanding. Community collaboration is especially good at getting information and wisdom directly from those affected rather than through an intermediary.

Pure community collaboration is adaptive work. It is more open, diverse, more free-form and emergent than day-to-day operational work. Its general goal is to capture or mine value from a collection of people who have assembled, often loosely, around some collaborative focal point, such as a shared interest, an idea, a concept, an opinion, a product design, a political position, a common experience, or a medical condition.

Where Community Collaboration Is Less Suitable

Community collaboration is less suitable for challenges that require deep analysis, where information is best provided by intermediaries who are often recognized experts and who influence one another. Also, if information is sensitive and requires significant safeguards in its use, then sharing it with the masses is less appropriate. A crowd is not particularly good at examining conflicting information and clearly separating fact from fiction. Gaining consensus and general agreement from a large group is also difficult, as is trying to improve something incrementally when that task requires deep knowledge of its inner workings.

Normally, such situations are better served by defined teams or groups working in accordance with a set of prescribed or established tasks, budgets, schedules, gates, workflows, rules, security, and decision authority. However, in some cases, such as Electronic Arts and CEMEX (as we discuss in chapters 8 and 9, respectively), the nature of the community and very-well-defined purposes can allow organizations to bring mass collaboration to challenges requiring deep analysis by a community of experts.

The gap between situations that are suitable for community collaboration and those that are not is actually a continuum. Rarely will an actual setting fall cleanly at one end or the other. A challenge needn't reside all the way to the right in figure 4-1 ("more suitable") in order to benefit from community collaboration. In most cases, the use of community collaboration will be a judgment call based on the particular goals and specific nature of the challenge. Also, to address the whole of an organizational challenge, you may need to blend community collaboration with some team collaboration and other forms of collaboration, communication, decision-making, and control techniques to create and sustain organizational change. You need to know when community collaboration must be augmented with other forms of execution.

To counteract aspects that make a situation less suitable for community collaboration, you can add some process or function controls. For example, Wikipedia struggled in the beginning to resolve conflicting information and ascertain facts because it lacked control structures. To deal with this problem, Wikipedia's leadership formulated a set of rules that define what constitutes an acceptable article and attracted a community of more than one thousand editors to interpret and enforce the rules. In the same way, although YouTube provides open information, it must still cope with copyright issues, which require some controls. The same applies to Facebook and privacy. In fact, most social media environments must impose some level of information controls because few, if any, situations will allow completely open mass collaboration.

Know Where Community Collaboration Is More Likely to Deliver Value

When creating a vision and strategy, you should understand generally where organizations tend to succeed with community collaboration. Many organizations have begun monitoring the social Web to understand emerging communities and trends that may impact their business. Some also collect and analyze information (or have a service provider do it) to track their Web reputation. Web reputation management may not apply to all organizations in all industries but, in general, social organizations "listen" to what is happening on the social Web to continuously assess its impact on their vision and strategy. This can help you determine how you might engage with existing communities rather than try to grow your own (more on this in chapter 7).

Through 2009 and 2010, we examined over four hundred cases from the United States (88 percent) and Europe (12 percent) to determine basic patterns in how firms employ social media to create business value. We culled this number to over two hundred cases in which community collaboration was the main objective (versus marketing communications, employee communications, team collaboration, and so on). Here are some of the findings.[4]

By Industry. We found some community collaboration adoption across many industries, with industries clearly falling into three distinct tiers of activity. The highest adoption tier comprises retail, government, media, IT, and consumer products. Each of these industries represented about 12 to 13 percent of the cases we found. These are the early adopters that have achieved success.

A second tier with notable adoption includes banking and finance, transportation, health care, pharmaceuticals, and manufacturing. Each represented 5 to 6 percent of the cases.

The third tier, with low levels of adoption, includes hospitality and travel, education, food and beverage, chemical, construction and engineering, electronics, energy, insurance, metals and natural resources, professional services, and utilities.

By Target Audience. Just over half of the cases were directed externally at communities of customers, prospects, constituents, and the like. More than a third targeted workforce-facing communities that included employees, contractors, or alumni. And the remaining cases, about 10 percent, targeted supply chain and service delivery partners.

By Source of Business Value.[5] We assigned each case to one or more of seven categories of business value. *Sales effectiveness* and *operational effectiveness* were the leaders; each was the goal in almost 40 percent of all cases. *Customer responsiveness*, *market responsiveness*, and *product/ service development* were the goals in about 20 percent of cases. In virtually no cases were the goals to improve *supplier effectiveness* or *regulatory responsiveness*.

By Business Use. We assigned the cases to the various business reasons for which firms use mass collaboration to gain business value. *Brand loyalty*, at 18 percent, was the most widespread use of community collaboration. *Customer service*, *operations execution*, *product/service delivery*, *product/service utilization*, *product/service engineering*, and *human relations* each represented between 7 and 12 percent of all cases. *Social learning*, *driving innovation*, *project management*, and *sales execution* showed less activity, with each under 5 percent of cases. The diversity of business-use cases where community collaboration has demonstrated value is notable. It reveals social media to be an enabler of positive change in many areas of business operations.

By Type of Mass Collaboration. In chapter 2 we described the kinds of mass collaboration that communities perform using social media. We examined adoption patterns by these types and found that *collective intelligence* and *expertise location* were the dominant types of mass collaboration at 67 percent and 50 percent, respectively. *Interest cultivation* at 26 percent and *relationship leverage* at 15 percent made up a second tier. *Mass coordination* and *emergent structures* were less mature and appeared in less than 5 percent of all cases each.

Apply an Understanding of Your Organization's Goals and Culture

To advance community collaboration from one-off incremental success to a transformational competence, an organization must use community collaboration to further its basic goals and strategies. This is the key way that collaboration will deliver substantial business value.

Creating explicit, strong links between community collaboration and organizational goals will immediately transform social media from an inconvenient, technology-hyped distraction to an important tool for enterprise success. Several important benefits flow from such links:

- They let you capitalize on existing organizational support for your goals, including potential champions at several levels and existing infrastructure around established programs and projects

- They help assure senior executive attention, which can prove invaluable in obtaining adequate funding and other resources

- They help combat the detrimental perception that social media is a "technology thing" rather than a business effort

Even if you don't have an official set of organizational goals, it's important to develop a shared understanding of what's important to the future success of the company. Look for community collaboration opportunities in these goals.

It's also important, even at this early stage, to take note of organizational and target community culture and how it might affect the adoption of community collaboration. *Culture* refers to the shared beliefs, norms, and values held by members of a group, including those who will participate in collaborative communities. Culture is an important aspect of the context in which you'll be operating.

For example, if information sharing and collaboration in general aren't valued, you will need to take extra steps to encourage participation in any collaborative communities you create. Culture should influence where and how you choose to focus your efforts. Be prepared to strike a balance between your ambitions for community collaboration and cultural realities. Culture is complex and can vary radically among disparate geographies, educational groups, industries, organizational levels, job roles, and even organizational units. You need to look at the culture of the organization and the target community and assess the risk of adoption.

However, we have found in our work that, though culture matters, there are no hard-and-fast rules—such as, for example, that you should avoid certain countries or industries or types of people. We have found that purpose is paramount. If you can tap into a meaningful "What's in it for them?" you can cultivate a successful community from culturally challenging groups. The strength of the right purpose can significantly mitigate the risk associated with cultural attitudes. It isn't too early to begin addressing this challenge during vision formulation.

The "Six F" Model of Attitudes Toward Social Media

Our research has uncovered a spectrum of six basic organizational attitudes—folly, fearful, flippant, formulating, forging, and fusing—about social media.[6] These *six F's* can play an important role in the success of your collaboration efforts. In fact, the attitudes within a large organization will most likely vary across units. Be sure to identify and understand this variation.

Folly

People with a folly attitude mainly consider social media a source of entertainment with insignificant or no business value. Leaders with this attitude usually ignore social media. However, because the organization doesn't actively prohibit it, business value can come from grassroots movements that capitalize on technologies readily available in the public space. The organization offers no guidance about how employees or others in its value chain might participate.

Where a folly attitude prevails, your vision must emphasize direct, specific business value. Avoid nebulous value statements around improved collaboration and stronger relationships. Instead, target tangible business benefits tied explicitly to well known and recognized organizational goals or challenges.

Fearful

Where fear of social media predominates, people see it primarily as a threat to productivity, intellectual capital, privacy, management authority, or regulatory compliance. With this attitude, the organization often does take a specific stance: it discourages and even prohibits the use of social media. This approach reduces the potential for undesirable behavior—that's the reason for restriction—but it also stifles any business value that might be derived from grassroots use of social media.

To counteract fear, the community collaboration vision should focus on relatively low-risk initiatives, even if other, higher-risk opportunities might offer greater business value.

Flippant

With a flippant attitude, people no longer fear social media, but they don't take it seriously either. Companies taking this approach simply make social media technology available, with some basic policy guidance, in hopes that productive communities will form spontaneously and deliver value to the organization. As we've already pointed out, this approach rarely succeeds. Organizations with a flippant approach treat social media and community collaboration as tactical rather than strategic.

The chief information officer (CIO) at a large investment firm in the United Kingdom indicated that it was just completing a policy covering the use of social media. When pressed about how he planned to move the organization from reactive and tactical efforts to more proactive and strategic approaches, he said, "Social media is like spreadsheets. I have no idea how they might use them. So my job is to provide the technology and some policy on their use." Unfortunately, this sentiment is rampant within IT departments. This organization is moving out of the fear stage and into the flippant stage, where the worst practice of provide-and-pray thrives.

Flippant organizations tend to treat social media as a technology platform rather than an enabler of business solutions. Unless this attitude shifts, they will find it very difficult to elevate community collaboration to a strategic opportunity. A well-formed and clearly expressed community collaboration vision will go a long way toward overcoming a flippant attitude. It will clearly show that leaders of the organization believe a strategic approach to social media can deliver substantial business value.

Formulating

With this attitude, organizational leadership recognizes both the value of community collaboration and the need to be more organized and strategic in its use. In almost all cases that we've seen, organizations have arrived at the formulating stage after progressing through the flippant provide-and-pray approach with little to no success. Simply providing access to social media technologies now gives way to active planning targeted at well-defined purposes.

For an organization at this stage, the social media vision should emphasize the strategic value of community collaboration, recognize the importance of sanctioned grassroots efforts, and position these steps as the beginning of an effort to build a strong organizational competency in collaboration.

Forging

In an organization with a forging attitude, people are beginning to integrate productive community collaboration into their daily work lives. But not just individuals are doing this—the whole organization is starting to develop competence in assembling, nurturing, and gaining business value from communities using social computing to collaborate. A forging organization is on its way to becoming a social organization. Successful and repeatable practices are emerging, and it's time to evolve them into a full-blown organizational competence. Business value has been proved, and leaders are eager to expand these efforts.

When an organization has a forging attitude, the vision statement should recognize previous successes and capitalize on growing momentum. It should advocate continued evolution and highlight investments already made and being made to drive toward the goal of becoming a social organization.

Fusing

Fusing is the most advanced attitude, and it is rare. Fusing organizations treat community collaboration as an integral part of their work; it's ingrained in how they think and behave. This is the attitude of a social organization, and in social organizations the need for an explicit vision and strategy subsides. All business strategy and execution already includes community collaboration wherever appropriate.

One of our goals is to help you avoid or counteract the folly, fear, and flippant attitudes and move directly to formulating and forging, where the strategic value of community collaboration is widely recognized.

Craft an Organizational Vision
for Community Collaboration

It's critical to involve the right people in vision formulation. This must be a business-led effort. The team involved needs to include business leaders from the major business units, especially those who already believe in the benefits of community collaboration. These leaders will ensure that the focus stays on business benefits. Talking technology too early in the process is a fundamental and often catastrophic error. The CIO and key staff should participate, of course, but social media should not be managed as a technology effort. Let us be clear: *if IT alone leads the effort, you have already stepped off the path to success*. Business leadership is crucial. Ideally, business leaders won't just participate; one will actually lead the development of a vision for community collaboration.

When your organization develops its vision for community collaboration, it sets the stage and emphasizes the focus on business value by reviewing organizational goals and strategies. Even go so far as posting them on the wall. Remind everyone that community collaboration may prove appropriate only for some of the goals. Your aim in this meeting is, first, to identify those goals where collaboration is appropriate and, second, to articulate at high levels how community collaboration can foster progress toward achieving them. In addition to goals, you can use major business activities and known significant collaboration challenges to spur brainstorming.

Once the enterprise goals, major activities, and/or collaboration challenges are identified and posted for all to see, employ a "People-Concerns-People" exercise to generate ideas. See figure 4-2 for a partial example of this approach, which was taken by NASA's Marshall Space Flight Center leadership.

Considering organizational objectives, list the associated concerns. Concerns are often of three types: known collaboration challenges, current business goals, or major business processes/activities (this last is reflected in the MSFC example). Then list the groups of people involved on both sides of that concern—the *doers* and the

FIGURE 4-2

"People-Concerns-People" brainstorming tool for NASA MSFC

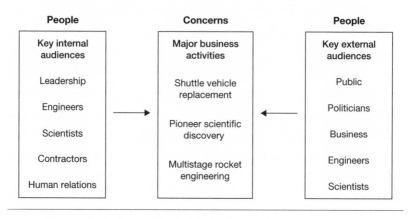

People	Concerns	People
Key internal audiences	Major business activities	Key external audiences
Leadership	Shuttle vehicle replacement	Public
Engineers		Politicians
Scientists	Pioneer scientific discovery	Business
Contractors	Multistage rocket engineering	Engineers
Human relations		Scientists

beneficiaries. List the internal groups relevant to the concern on the left and the external groups on the right. Then ask, "How can community collaboration within and among these groups add value to one or more of the concerns listed in the middle?" Reviewing the types of mass collaboration behaviors introduced in chapter 2 (collective intelligence, expertise location, emergent structures, mass coordination, interest cultivation, and relationship leverage) can help the people in the room think more concretely and help generate ideas and discussion.

As MSFC's leaders at NASA discussed the application of community collaboration to three major organizational activities, they began identifying the primary people involved and brainstorming ideas for how mass collaboration could help. For example: How might engineers and scientists within MSFC collaborate with engineers outside the organization on designing a replacement vehicle for the space shuttle? How might MSFC leaders, engineers, and scientists collaborate with private businesses to pioneer scientific discovery and increase MSFC's overall value to the world?

The goal at this stage is to develop a set of *community collaboration opportunity statements* that capture where community collaboration can support the success of your organization. We recommend sticking closely to a specific format for each opportunity area and including this information: *Who, collaborating around what, will deliver what benefits to themselves and what value to the organization?* The *who* are the target community participants who collaborate around some tangible, concrete purpose that delivers obvious benefits to both participants and the organization. Here is an example set of opportunity statements created through brainstorming for inclusion in the MSFC's organizational vision.[7]

- "Enabling MSFC science and engineering teams to collaborate with the general public on design innovations. This will help close the duration gap between the current shuttle program and the replacement vehicle program."

- "Enabling MSFC's workforce, leadership, and HR to collaborate around the transition of skills and knowledge from the shuttle program to future programs/projects or other potential efforts. We can reuse shuttle program expertise, ease employee job transitions, and ensure continued mission execution excellence."

- "Empowering MSFC engineers and managers to continuously collaborate with each other and with partners on engineering designs for products that cross engineering stages. We can drive higher-quality designs, shorten project timelines, and lower project costs."

- "Creating a community where MSFC engineers, scientists, public relations department, and the general public (public scientists and technologists) collaborate on industry utilization of NASA inventions. The goal is to drive worldwide technology evolution/invention and promote NASA's general contribution to science and technology."

The brainstorming session should produce several draft opportunity statements. Be strategic. Look for areas that you feel will have a significant impact on your greatest challenges. The opportunity statements can represent a mix of employee-facing, customer-facing, supplier-facing, market-facing, or even general public–facing communities, depending on the goals and focus of the organization. At the same time, always be sure that community collaboration is a genuine part of the solution. But the statements should not address specific social media channels or technologies. Leave the details of the solution to subsequent activities. These draft statements will provide the material for the final community collaboration vision.

To clean up what came from brainstorming and craft the final vision, winnow down the statements to a coherent and manageable set. Eliminate duplication. Combine those that are similar and make sense when merged. Brainstorming can be messy, and so you may have statements not truly based on community collaboration. Others may not be desirable to pursue for some self-evident reason. For example, eliminate those that aren't really feasible or present significant risks. Prioritize the remaining statements, and link them clearly to organization goals. Choose some to include in the vision that represent the term (short, medium, or long) you are targeting in the vision. Write all this up, do a final review, and distribute the vision statement.

As we pointed out earlier, a vision statement may not be necessary for a full-fledged social organization because mass collaboration will simply be "the way we do business." But in the early days, collaborative communities need both the broad endorsement and the specificity of the vision statement we've described. It's a necessary step on the road to becoming a social organization.

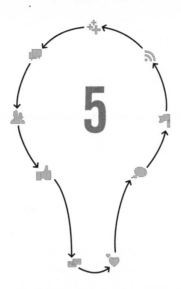

Developing a Strategic Approach to Community Collaboration

A global leader in selling, marketing, and distributing food products to restaurants, hospitals, schools, and other organizations had grown significantly through acquisition to well over one hundred distributors.

In 2010 the company's leadership recognized that social media was being used across the organization among employees and between employees and customers. They knew of some successes and some failures in these efforts but, in fact, they knew little about how their organization was really applying social media or its effect on the business. They saw it as both a potential risk and a major opportunity, and wanted to maximize the opportunity and minimize the risk. Realizing success wouldn't just happen on its own, they began to take a proactive approach and build a strategy.

At the same time, they also recognized the power of grassroots communities and didn't want to stifle innovation among distributors. In fact, they wanted to leverage distributors' social media successes by quickly propagating them to other distributors.

Thus an important part of the company's strategy was to encourage valuable grassroots efforts while pursuing top-down community collaboration initiatives.

The company's two-pronged approach is a social organization best practice, and in this chapter we examine how to achieve the right mix of both intelligently and strategically.

Chances are high that people in your organization are already using social media, a trend that is almost certain to grow with or without your permission or support. No matter what you say they can or cannot do, employees go outside the organization to participate in such environments as LinkedIn and Facebook and to access software as a service (SaaS) in the cloud, where they create their own social environments—all of which creates two problems: they expose the organization to potential risk, and the organization misses an opportunity to make community collaboration a valuable corporate competence.

How are you dealing with this inevitability? Some organizations ignore it. Some try to squelch it. Some write policies to contain it. But social organizations build a strategy to tap into it for business gain.

Setting a vision for community collaboration, which we discussed in chapter 4, is the first step in gaining some control. A vision tells people community collaboration is valued and will be actively pursued. Publishing a vision is likely to unleash a flood of ideas from people throughout the organization for new social media uses. And it will surface existing community collaboration environments looking for corporate validation.

You will need to blend the top-down efforts identified in your vision statement with bottom-up grassroots efforts. Since you cannot and should not try to do everything, you will need to decide which community collaboration efforts should move forward and which should not. Making these choices is the function of the strategy portion of our approach.

What Is a Community Collaboration Strategy?

An organizational strategy for community collaboration explicitly identifies the communities the firm will investigate, sanction, and support; when and how it will support them; the desired collaborative behaviors they will exhibit; and the organizational benefits expected to flow from them. As we explain in this chapter, you should employ a portfolio management approach in making strategy and investment decisions on community collaboration efforts.

Building the strategy involves two main activities. The first is establishing the means to intelligently select, from the multitude of community collaboration possibilities, those that you should pursue. The second is determining where and when to invest, or continue investing, in specific collaborative communities.

Include in these activities *all* your community collaboration efforts. Whatever target audience, geography, industry, or other subset you choose, the strategy steps outlined here apply just the same.

Strategy always begins with purpose. Indeed, it is planning based on purpose because purpose provides the intelligence you need to choose wisely. Purpose drives all other strategy considerations. Social organizations understand the central role of purpose. Nothing is more important to success.

The Importance of Purpose

"Try out this new community so you can work more collaboratively, faster, and with higher quality."

If you received this message from your boss, would you jump at the chance to participate? Probably not.

"Collaborate with other people in {your town} around our products so we can serve you better."

If you got this notice from a local business, would you be moved to join in? Not likely.

Yet organizations pursue community collaboration with general, bland invitations like these and then are disappointed to find they get poor, if any, adoption. Managers interested in social media often ask, "How can we get our knowledge workers to collaborate more to do better work?" Not by merely providing the technology. And not with an uninviting and easily forgettable purpose. To succeed, you must go deeper and define specifically what you want people to collaborate around and why.

People need a compelling cause. Their contribution must have a purpose, and that purpose must be meaningful to them, or they won't participate. Without a targeted, specific, and engaging purpose, participation is unlikely. If people come together, it will be only because the community has found its own purpose. This seems like a good thing, and it may be. But it may not be. Will that random purpose align with corporate goals? Who knows? Without a purpose that people find compelling *and* that provides specific organizational benefits, business value will be left to chance and, worse, the community may even create unnecessary risk for the organization.

Here's an example: a professional services firm provided consultants with a social networking tool to improve collaboration and coordination. Yet management provided no guidance about why or how the consultants should collaborate because it didn't want to constrain them. Management wanted to see what collaborative benefits would arise spontaneously.

What arose was essentially a corporate dating site. Female consultants began complaining to HR because male consultants were using the tool to find potential dates. HR threw up a red flag, and the firm shut down the social networking environment. As a consequence, those in the organization who opposed social media had the ammunition to block other community collaboration efforts, which set the firm back significantly in comparison with the capabilities some of its competitors were developing.

This effort did not fail for lack of purpose. A purpose did emerge, but not one aligned with the general goal. The effort failed for lack of a strategy. The firm didn't clarify a desired purpose for the community and the benefits it expected the community to produce.

Another example went differently. A global professional services firm realized it was missing a significant opportunity to derive maximum benefit from its work with clients. Thousands of consultants were developing new products and services for clients, but the consultants had no way to identify other clients around the world who needed the same products and services. Conversely, thousands of other consultants who knew their clients' needs didn't know the firm had already created a product or service that would meet those needs. The firm wanted to drive new business by facilitating a community of consultants who collaborated around connecting client needs with capabilities anywhere in the company.

To address this purpose, leadership asked those consultants responsible for both managing large projects and finding new business to create three profiles: one of their team and its offerings, one of work being done for clients, and one of client needs. The firm then used both social network analysis technology and manual search technology to make connections between consultants. The firm was able to track the number of automated connections, the number of manual connections, how many connections led to a proposal, and how such proposals led to new business. Because the purpose was clear and specific, the firm could target and measure business value.

A well-formed purpose addresses a recognized problem and is specific enough to motivate an identifiable target audience to participate. It also clearly articulates the benefits to community members and the business value to the organization. No longer than a paragraph, it answers four basic questions:

- Who are the target participants?

- What is the nature or focus of their collaboration?

- What's in it for participants?

- What value will the organization realize?

Purpose statements are similar in format to the opportunity statements you developed while creating an organizational vision for community collaboration. The main difference is in granularity. Opportunity statements are more general and describe a business possibility, whereas purpose statements are more specific to a community (versus an area of the business) and are intended to resonate strongly with members of that community.

Here are three well-formed purpose statements from different industries and geographies that address different audiences (customers, employees, and partners):

Engage customers of our XXX product to collaborate on innovative uses of the product to enhance their value from and enjoyment of the product, increase customer loyalty, and provide us with critical information for product evolution. (U.S.-based consumer electronics company)

Engage our mechanical engineers throughout the world to collaborate on solving our current automotive parts product issues concerning performance in high-stress environments (heat and sand) to improve product performance, decrease costly failures, and increase customer satisfaction. (Europe-based automotive parts company that serves the defense industry, among others)

Engage watershed managers across the United States to share best practices in gaining local citizen involvement in executing on their watershed management plans to improve water quality and increase local pride in watershed management.[1] (U.S. Environmental Protection Agency's Watershed Management community)

You can determine the power and potential value of a purpose by assessing it against the following characteristics:[2]

- *Magnetic:* The purpose should naturally draw people to participate. This is the "What's in it for me?" factor. If you have to create interest, especially through costly incentives, then you've chosen the wrong purpose.

- *Business-aligned:* The purpose should have a clear alignment with business goals. This is the "What's in it for the business?" factor.

- *Low community risk:* Choose low risk over high reward. The purpose, especially early in an organization's use of community collaboration, should not run against the grain of the current culture in the community or the company. Do not try to change culture with social software. This is rampant bad practice. No matter how enticing the business reward, always focus first on driving participation.

- *Measurable:* You should be able to measure the success of a good purpose. Especially in the beginning, when people in your organization might be more skeptical of social media, choose purposes where business and community value can be clearly and tangibly assessed.

- *Facilitates evolution:* Select purposes that you and the community can build on. Some purposes more naturally tend to foster emergence and lead to other purposes. (We'll return to this important criterion in chapter 6.)

A high-quality purpose will have all these characteristics.

Empower Community Collaboration with the "No, Go, Grow" Model

New purposes can come top-down from leaders as an organization explicitly pursues opportunities identified in its vision statement for community collaboration. Purposes can also rise bottom-up from employees or even customers. They can also emerge from existing communities. With purposes coming from all directions, you need a way to gather, assess, and make decisions about which purposes to forgo, which to pursue, and which to explore further. How do you decide which purposes to green light? And any decision to move ahead will require yet another: once you decide to pursue a collaboration effort, you must decide how to proceed. Can a collaborative community succeed as a grassroots effort? If not, does it merit corporate investment and the ongoing time and attention of management?

To make these strategic decisions, we offer the *No, Go, Grow* decision model (see figure 5-1), a way of systematically determining if and how a community collaboration effort should move forward.[3]

FIGURE 5-1

The "No, Go, Grow" decision model for community collaboration

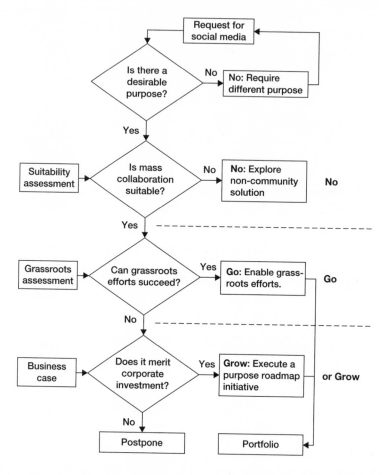

Source: Anthony J. Bradley, "Use a Gartner Governance Model to More Safely Empower Grassroots Social Media Efforts," Gartner Inc., October 9, 2009.

Although we depict the model as a linear flowchart, you can loop back at any point if more information is needed for a decision.

The No Stage

The No stage is the first hurdle every proposed collaborative community must get over—both those identified in the original vision statement and those subsequently proposed by people and groups in the organization. The key questions in this stage are: "Is there a clear and desirable purpose for the community?" and "Is mass collaboration appropriate for the purpose and the community?"

Social media–based efforts very often start with a request for technology. When someone says, "I need a wiki," respond by asking, "Why do you want a wiki? What's your purpose?" If there is no purpose, send the requester back to the drawing board and help her articulate why she needs a wiki (or any other social technology).

If a grassroots-driven social media community already exists, explore and evaluate the underlying purposes around which the community has formed. With a little corporate support, it could be a significant asset for the firm.

But, whatever the source of the idea for the community, if it lacks a well-formed purpose or has an undesirable one, it should produce a No, in which case it may have to be shut down or guided to improve its purpose.

Once a clear and desirable purpose is in hand, you can then decide if community collaboration is the right approach. To help with this assessment, use the suitability model shown in figure 4-1. If the purpose merits a No, the organization can explore other non-mass collaboration–based solutions. If community collaboration is suitable, take the purpose to the Go stage.

The Go Stage

The decision to *Go* hinges on whether a potential collaborative community is likely to succeed on its own as a grassroots effort or with minimal organizational support. If a grassroots effort's chances of success are acceptable, the organization gives it a Go and provides, or continues to provide, access to social media technology. If the community is already under way, it becomes a recognized, approved, and monitored collaborative community. In both instances, it becomes part of the organization's community collaboration portfolio.

The assessment and approval of grassroots collaborative communities is critical to becoming a social organization. Why? Because grassroots communities substantially increase the pace of transformation and create a culture that values community collaboration. An organization can invest in only so many top-down efforts. In addition, pursuing only top-down initiatives creates a "wait to be told what to do" culture that is counter to the spirit of the collaboration movement.

In a fully developed social organization, the number of approved and monitored grassroots communities may be orders of magnitude higher than the number of top-down efforts. But top-down efforts are crucial to showing the way and building momentum. And top-down efforts are often the ones with the most impact on the business because they are more closely linked to specific enterprise goals. A social organization blends top-down and grassroots efforts in its community collaboration portfolio.

Note the significant difference between a Go decision and the provide-and-pray practice we cautioned against in chapter 3. With provide-and-pray, the organization provides access to social media technology without understanding how it will be used. A Go decision, however, is made only after determining that:

1. A well-formed, desirable purpose exists

2. The purpose is suitable for social media and mass collaboration

3. The characteristics of the purpose suggest strongly that a grassroots effort can succeed primarily on its own

What are the characteristics that indicate a collaborative community can succeed on its own as a grassroots effort? The following will help you determine if a collaborative community is likely to coalesce and succeed on its own:[4]

- Community formation

- Participation magnetism

- Investment needs

- Management involvement

- Policy and security

The importance of each criterion will vary, depending on a proposed community's purpose and the organization's priorities.

Community Formation. How difficult will it be to form a community? To determine this, ask:

- Is the community readily identifiable?

- Does the community already exist offline?

- Does the community already exist online?

- Is there a history of collaboration?

- Is the culture of the target community already conducive to community collaboration and social media?

A grassroots community has a greater chance of success if the community already exists and is already collaborating, and simply needs a better set of technology tools.

Without an already-existing community, you must assess how clearly the potential community can be identified and how natural it will be for its members to collaborate. Is it likely they'll coalesce around the purpose? Do they share an interest in the purpose, even if that interest comes from different points of view? A clearly identified community of members who seem likely to share interests increases the odds of grassroots success.

A preexisting culture of collaboration will increase the chances of success with a grassroots-driven effort.

Even if the target community is well defined, the lack of a collaborative culture and a history of interaction may flag the community as an adoption risk. For a grassroots effort to take hold, the target community must have an inclination for, or at least minimal resistance to, broader collaboration and social media. People who have a history of hoarding information or preferring to work in silos are not good grassroots candidates. If you must take proactive measures to overcome cultural resistance, then the community is not appropriate for a grassroots effort and is likely to fail if you treat it as one. To get at this important aspect, ask: Will participants be naturally motivated, or will they require incentives to join in? Will social incentives, such as status in the community, be sufficient? Or will external incentives be required?

The need for incentives—such as awards, prizes, bonuses, recognition, performance evaluations, and marketing efforts—is inconsistent with grassroots movements. Communities that require them will also require leadership involvement, organizational investment, and change management, which are evaluated as part of the Grow decision.

Compatibility with existing organizational practices and systems will increase the chances of success with a grassroots community effort.

How comfortable and familiar will the target community be with the kind of social interaction required to achieve its purpose? In some groups, such behaviors may conflict with existing practices and systems. As a result, target members may be reluctant to participate because of simple aversion to change, confusion over what is acceptable behavior, fear of breaking rules, preference for existing practice, avoidance of perceived duplication of effort, and a host of other reasons.

Compare the behavior necessary to achieve the purpose with current practices and systems. The closer the alignment, the higher the chances of success—because unless there is widespread and strong dissatisfaction with the status quo, changing people's behavior is difficult. Greater change requires greater investment in new systems. In general, the bigger the departure from established practices, the larger the investment required. A significant investment is more consistent with making a Grow decision and a top-down approach.

Participation Magnetism. Magnetism is the natural attractiveness of a collaborative community's purpose to potential participants. A highly magnetic purpose will increase the chances of success in any community, but it's mandatory for a grassroots effort. Potential community members must easily understand what's in it for them and feel a strong draw to participate. This mitigates the need for external incentives or extensive marketing, seeding, leadership, and other investments more associated with top-down initiatives.

Questions to ask here include: How strongly will the purpose resonate with the target audience? Will audience members recognize immediately how participation will benefit them? Is the purpose an inspiring cause around which a community will naturally rally? Is the purpose compelling enough that it will spark contagion?

Contagious or viral membership growth—what happens when a purpose is so compelling that members recruit other participants—is a result of strong magnetism. A social media purpose that is somewhat magnetic but lacks the potential for creating contagious growth can still succeed. But it will require marketing investments in advertising, events, incentives, and the like, which will make it more suited for some level of top-down support. For a grassroots community to succeed on its own, its purpose must inspire contagious membership.

For example, a large U.S. publishing company whose computing systems were primarily mainframe faced a situation where many of its IT employees were approaching retirement. This was a potential problem because the company's mainframe applications were largely undocumented, which meant the company depended on knowledge that existed only in those workers' heads. The company installed a wiki and asked the employees to document the details of the applications. However, employees didn't see "What's in it for me?" in that purpose, so they didn't contribute. Some even thought they might retire and then do contract work with the company. The company's purpose in the wiki was not magnetic enough to generate grassroots participation. To fulfill the purpose, the company would need to offer an exit bonus to those who contributed content at acceptable quantity and quality levels. This challenge requires top-down involvement; now, following its provide-and-pray failure, the company is reevaluating the effort.

Investment Needs. As you assess a potential grassroots community, look carefully at how much investment in money, effort, and other resources it will require. Grassroots efforts are expected by their nature to make progress with no or minimal corporate investment.

The need for capital investment in IT infrastructure will decrease the chances of grassroots success.

Social websites such as Facebook, YouTube, and Twitter, along with SaaS-based social software tools, are major enablers of grassroots communities. They provide easy-to-deploy and often inexpensive access to social media environments and technologies. Also, some internal efforts start with modest means. For example, Best Buy's Blue Shirt Nation, a robust community of Best Buy employees who convene regularly to share knowledge, best practices, frustrations, aspirations, and a few jokes, succeeded as an on-premises implementation started by two employees with a single server under one of their desks.[5]

However, if building and launching a collaborative community will require capital investment in infrastructure scalability, reliability, or flexibility, it's not suitable as a grassroots effort. Organizational infrastructure investment is more consistent with a top-down approach.

A significant requirement for system integration will reduce a grassroots community's chances of success.

A grassroots effort that requires even modest integration with existing organizational systems such as customer relationship management (CRM), content-management, and workflow systems is less likely to succeed. While recent technological developments have made integration less complex, community participants normally lack the will, access, resources, or skills to undertake the job themselves.

A need for integration with existing systems suggests a need for technology support and organizational investment more suited for a top-down effort.

A significant requirement for content seeding will reduce the chances of success with a grassroots-driven effort.

A community environment must provide immediate value to participants. This means content and interactions must be available before significant adoption will occur. In a successful grassroots effort, a subset of early-adopter participants will themselves populate the environment with content and activity that will attract "mass adopters." In short, the community itself provides from the beginning all the value that will lead to mass adoption.

If a community will require critical seeding of starter content by the organization prior to adoption then it probably won't succeed as a grassroots effort. For example, with http://www.regulations.gov/exchange/, the U.S. government had to seed the site with regulations before community participants could contribute feedback about those regulations. The community could not be productive without this content and they could not post it themselves. Therefore, because upfront effort was required to get this content into the environment, it wasn't suitable to be treated as a grassroots effort.

Management Involvement. For a bottom-up effort to succeed, it must provide its own leadership.

The need for outside leadership will reduce the odds that a grassroots-driven effort can succeed.

Understanding whether, where, and to what degree indigenous leadership is needed and will appear is important in assessing the possible long-term success of a grassroots effort. To get at such issues, ask questions like these: What is the need for leadership? Where will leadership come from in the formulation and growth of this community? Are there grassroots leaders who can rally others, guide behaviors, champion the purpose, and otherwise further the goal and facilitate results? Will organizational managers need to champion and participate for the program to succeed?

If a grassroots community requires more than minimal leadership from outside the community, then by definition it's not really a grassroots movement.

A direct alignment between business goals and member benefits will increase the chances of success with a grassroots effort.

There's always the possibility that any collaborative community, but especially a grassroots community, will form and thrive but not deliver any business value. To succeed, a grassroots community must be both valuable to community members and productive for the organization. So it's important to ask of a grassroots effort: Will value to the enterprise materialize here with little or no organizational involvement?

The answer is more likely to be positive when the benefits to the community are the same as, or closely aligned with, the benefits to the organization. For example, an environment where engineers collaborate to solve design challenges benefits both participants personally and the organization. This kind of direct alignment will make the measurement of business value much easier.

However, a grassroots effort where benefits are not aligned— where benefits to participants and to the organization are not the same—can be problematic. For example, Procter & Gamble provides a community where young women can share experiences around coming of age.[6] The benefit to the participants is personal support, while the value to P&G comes from branding and marketing benefits. The benefits to the community are indirectly aligned to the benefits for P&G. Because of this indirect alignment, P&G marketing must be involved to find ways of deriving organization benefits from community interactions.

Policy and Security. Every human community, online or not, runs the risk of bad behavior by members. This risk can take two forms: the risk of dysfunctional behavior that destroys or limits the ability of the community to collaborate, and the risk that members' actions will expose the organization to legal action, loss of proprietary information, or damage to its reputation.

In either case—dysfunctional, antisocial behavior or breaches of security—a high level of risk will decrease the chances that a grassroots effort can succeed.

The more damaging the possible consequences—for example, the loss of information linked to competitive advantage—the greater the need for governance. You must assess the purpose and target community involved in a grassroots effort to determine the potential for bad behavior and its level of risk. (See chapter 10 for a more in-depth look at governance.)

A high potential for risk will present real problems. A grassroots community is likely to respond negatively to restrictions, since grassroots communities typically prefer to be self-governing. If the potential for bad behavior is initially high, the community will need help encouraging good and discouraging bad behavior. This effort often involves tools, along with people to moderate community interactions. Again, if a community requires that level of governance, it's less appropriate for a grassroots effort.

You may want to avoid altogether any grassroots efforts that create and share sensitive information. Information security, assurance, privacy protection, and other regulatory requirements demand a top-down approach. Few organizations are willing to leave security management to community participants, even for moderate security risks.

If risks are high, the purpose may not be suitable for a community collaboration approach of any kind. Some organizations use security and policy as a general rationale for stifling all or most community collaboration; they make little or no effort to do a risk-return assessment. Others believe that if they can mitigate the risk, they will gain competitive advantage. But those that do take on the challenge don't leave security management to grassroots efforts.

One of the most high-profile, successful government collaboration efforts is the Intellipedia effort created by the U.S. intelligence community. Intellipedia lets thousands of intelligence analysts across sixteen organizations share information. Started in 2005, Intellipedia after four years housed over 900,000 pages edited by 100,000 users.[7] If the U.S. intelligence community focused only on risk, then this essential means of coordinating important information would never have gotten off the ground.

When you assess grassroots movements, you'll rarely find the situation clear-cut, and you must apply judgment case-by-case. After assessing the five criteria, make a Go or Grow decision. Purposes that can succeed as grassroots efforts with minimal management or organizational investment (other than providing social media technology) are given the green light and added to the community collaboration portfolio as grassroots efforts. From that point, sanctioned grassroots efforts jump right to the launch stage of the community-cultivation cycle. Launch activities for them will normally be minimal because, by definition, all they need is access to an appropriate social media technology. (You will still need to determine the extent to which you will want or need to guide these communities after launch.)

The Grow Stage

A large construction company in Asia that specializes in office buildings and housing complexes was losing millions every year to materials spoilage. Quantities of overage materials would often remain at a site, exposed to the elements, until they were unusable. The company created a collaborative community where project managers (PMs) could sell their overstock materials to each other and share best practices in combating spoilage. The buying PM got materials cheaper than in the open market, and the selling PM didn't have to absorb the cost of spoilage. This was a solid purpose that would benefit both community participants and the company. However, the PMs lacked a culture of collaboration, and many were averse to IT and social media. In this situation, a high level of participation was necessary for the community to fulfill its purpose, and a grassroots approach would not get them there. So, with a top-down effort, the company targeted a subset of PMs who were more likely to participate and publicly recognized and even gave bonuses to some who did participate successfully. This attracted the attention of the more reluctant PMs, who began to participate. The company broke even on its community investment within the first year and hopes to decrease spoilage losses by 50 percent by the end of year two.

This is a good example of the need for incentives in coalescing a community where a grassroots approach is likely to fail. Those collaboration proposals that don't get the grassroots green light move into the *Grow* stage. A community purpose that moves to this stage is one that could deliver value to both community and organization, but only with more formal support. Here you must decide whether the purpose actually merits investment and a top-down community-building effort. An organization can invest in only a limited number of communities, and so this decision requires justification based on the goals and needs of the business. Some purposes may be outright rejected as not worth an investment.

Those Grow efforts moving forward go into the community collaboration portfolio as projects. A Grow assessment is just a decision to move a potential community collaboration effort forward as a top-down project. The execution of this top-down effort happens in the refine purpose phase of the community-cultivation cycle, which we will cover in chapter 6. Likewise, the No, Go, Grow decision process also feeds approved Go grassroots efforts into the portfolio and they move into the launch phase of the community-cultivation cycle (see figure 5-2).

FIGURE 5-2

Progressing from decision to portfolio to reality

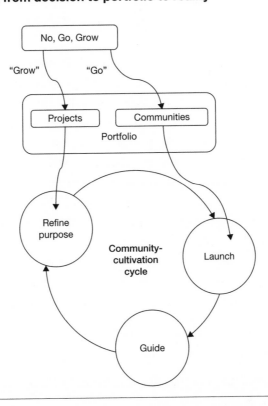

Managing the Community Collaboration Portfolio

Community collaboration portfolio management is a method for analyzing and collectively managing a group of current or proposed community collaboration efforts based on key characteristics.

The fundamental objective of portfolio management is to determine the optimal set, mix and sequencing of community collaboration efforts to achieve your organization's overall goals—typically expressed in terms of hard economic measures and business results—while honoring constraints imposed by management or external factors.

Most medium-sized and large companies already have a scattering of collaborative communities, but they're not documented and therefore not visible or managed as a whole. If you're serious about becoming a social organization with community collaboration as a core competence, you need to manage your social media efforts more formally as a coherent portfolio of purposeful communities. *The portfolio is the main outcome of an organization's community collaboration strategy.*

Taking a portfolio approach, which means you manage the set of community collaboration efforts as a group, not one by one, will help you deal with a diversity of issues. Where should your organization focus its efforts? Where is there overlap? You might be asking engineers to participate in two or three different communities that pursue two or three very different purposes. Is that a good thing? Might that overload them? If so, where should they focus? Only a portfolio-based approach will provide the overview required to treat community collaboration as a cost effective and efficient organizational capability.

Portfolio management involves tracking community collaboration efforts and their key characteristics across the organization in order to make such important investment decisions as:

- Which top-down community collaboration efforts get executed and when?

- What bottom-up grassroots collaborative communities get resources and how many?

- Which ongoing efforts get additional resources to expand on current success?

- What are the interdependencies between community collaboration efforts?

- Which ongoing efforts are not succeeding—and therefore should lose support?

- What areas of the business are light on community collaboration and deserve a deeper look at how it might deliver value there?

- Where does a proposed new community overlap with an existing effort, and how can the existing effort be leveraged?

- Is one target audience so saturated with community collaboration that it's a candidate for social media fatigue?

- Is community collaboration having a significant impact on the organization's success?

To answer these questions and make important decisions, maintain at least the following information in your portfolio for each collaborative community:

- Brief description of the community (including purposes)

- Target audience

- Whether it's top-down or grassroots-driven

- Maturity of the effort—how long has it been in place?

- Related organizational goal or objective

- Key dependencies

- Current investment (project funding or ongoing operations)

- Current success (in terms of the business measures used to justify its formation)

- Additional investment requested

- Additional investment justification

As we noted, *a portfolio of collaborative communities is the primary product of your efforts to develop a strategy for mass collaboration.* A portfolio approach enables you to manage investments in community collaboration as organizational capabilities and to influence what efforts move forward, their rate of change, and the impact on other business systems and operations. Your company can only tackle so much at once, and opening up the floodgates to community collaboration can create an undesirable and disruptive rate of change. Customers and employees usually have far more ideas for change than an organization can digest. Some of those ideas might also conflict with the organization's operating model and goal. Not all change is good change.

Portfolio management enables an organization to influence where change happens, when it happens, and how much happens. It's the key mechanism for balancing emergence and investment. The portfolio will evolve continuously. Social organizations consider such portfolio management to be a core competence. If your firm already possesses skills and processes for portfolio management—perhaps developed from managing an application portfolio—adapt and use them to manage your portfolio of collaborative communities.

The No, Go, Grow decision model will help you grow this portfolio intelligently. Go decisions add grassroots communities that, once approved, require little further effort other than guidance. Grow decisions represent strategic investment in top-down initiatives, which require more focused and vigorous efforts to decide if and how to proceed. That effort involves, for each proposed purpose and community, a purpose roadmap and a more formal business justification, both of which we will cover in chapter 6.

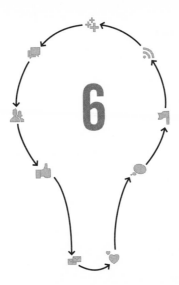

Refining Purpose by Building Purpose Roadmaps

A few years ago, a global religious organization set out to employ social media technologies to engage its members around various matters of concern to practicing Christians. Because this organization's membership consisted primarily of college and high school students, an ideal audience for social media, the chances of success seemed large.

As organizational leaders planned the community, they defined numerous purposes that would entice people to participate, such as:

Bible study: Participants share what the Bible means to them.

Mission work networking: Participants collaborate to find global missionary opportunities and share their experiences as missionaries.

Good works sharing: Participants collaborate to find local volunteer opportunities and share their experiences as volunteers.

Christian dating: Participants find like-minded people to build personal relationships.

Community assimilation: Participants help members who've relocated find a Christian community in their new locale.

Marriage preparation: Married participants help others prepare for matrimony.

Marriage support: Participants share experiences to help others navigate the challenges of marriage.

Grief support: Participants provide support and share grief experiences to help others through times of loss.

Job networking: Participants collaborate to help others find employment.

Christian growth: Participants share experience and advice for becoming a better Christian.

The planners were excited by the many ways they could use this technology to help members. They thought that the more purposes they built in, the more enticing the community would be, so they planned to implement all these purposes in the first version of the social media environment they were creating.

However, a variety of purposes implemented all at once creates enormous complexity. To include so many initially, the organization needed to design a multitude of different member experiences requiring a wide variety of technical functionality. Indeed, to support all those purposes required almost all social media functionality then available. In addition, the planners needed to seed the environment with content and expertise in multiple different areas. And they needed to market many different reasons for participation. Getting such a social environment off the ground would take years and hefty investment.

But cost and time aren't the only or even the biggest challenges created by complexity. The biggest problem is user adoption. Complexity can overwhelm and confuse potential participants: "Am I here to study the Bible, find a date, or get help with grieving?" Complexity creates a learning curve, and learning curves are unacceptable in community collaboration. Pursuing all these purposes at once violates Gall's Law: "Every successful complex system starts as a successful simple system." *Never break Gall's Law.* If you do, you can easily cripple community collaboration adoption.

In its enthusiasm, this organization went ahead with multiple purposes. It took the planners over two years to launch the project, and, once they did, adoption fell far short of expectations, in most areas attracting less than 10 percent of the target audience.

Having completed work on organizational vision and organizational strategy, you now have a portfolio of communities you plan to grow or, at least, investigate further. In the vision stage, you identified some as areas of opportunity in your organization where mass collaboration can produce value. Other communities in your portfolio will have arisen as unsolicited bottom-up requests. In the strategy stage, you ran both types of potential community through the No, Go, Grow decision model. Now your portfolio comprises those that survived the No hurdle and have been designated either Go communities (grassroots movements requiring little support or guidance) or Grow communities (those that are worth doing but require more investigation, preparation, and investment).

Now you will turn to designing and growing the *individual* collaborative communities in your portfolio.

In chapter 3 we introduced the community-cultivation cycle (repeated here in figure 6-1) as the means to prepare, launch, and sustain successful communities.

Given the importance of purpose in collaboration, you won't be surprised when we say that cultivating a community begins with, and is based on, its purpose. In this chapter we will describe and explore the two key activities that comprise the "Refine purpose" part of the diagram:

- First, you will expand the community's initial planned purpose, the cause it's intended to pursue, into a *purpose roadmap*.

- Second, you will develop a *business justification* that identifies the community's tangible business benefits and costs.

FIGURE 6-1

Community-cultivation cycle

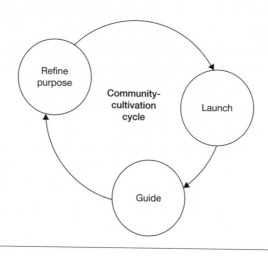

In both these activities, you will focus almost entirely on the communities you've decided to Grow. Because Grow communities need corporate investment, they require a purpose roadmap before they go on to launch. Though they must have a strong initial purpose, Go communities do not require a roadmap prior to launch. That's because a Go community, which by definition can succeed entirely as a grassroots movement, is expected to thrive on its initial purpose and evolve its own new purposes over time. You may decide to prepare a purpose roadmap to help guide a Go community's evolution but a roadmap isn't necessary to catalyze it. Nor will a Go community need business justification, because it will require virtually no investment, other than possibly some technical support in the launch phase (we'll discuss this in chapter 7). Go communities typically move quickly through launch where their needs for guidance and ongoing investment are usually minimal.

Why Create a Purpose Roadmap?

A purpose is a specific and meaningful reason for collaboration that will motivate members of a community to interact and contribute. The initial purpose of a Grow community can serve as the starting point, but alone it won't sustain a community over time. For that, you need a purpose roadmap.

As we noted in chapter 3, a purpose roadmap is a set of related and sequenced purposes that define how a community's collaboration can start, grow, and evolve.[1] It is a planning tool, your primary means to influence the future of a community. By identifying possible focal points for collaboration over time, a roadmap can serve as a guide for the development and growth of the community. It's particularly important at start-up because it lays out the possibilities for a community without overwhelming it in the beginning. This is what the Christian organization described at the opening of this chapter was missing when it planned its community.

A purpose roadmap is a plan but not a fixed, immutable plan. It defines what *might* or *could* be, not what necessarily *will* be. It suggests possibilities—sometimes strong possibilities, but always possibilities. In a thriving community, new purposes will emerge, while old purposes may be accomplished, adapted to new circumstances, or even lose relevance. As new purposes emerge and old ones may fade away, these changes are folded into the original roadmap, which becomes a continuously evolving picture of the community's possible future.

As a malleable plan for evolution, a purpose roadmap provides many benefits.

A purpose roadmap identifies the target community and how it may change over time. A purpose roadmap provides the context for understanding who the participants are, what motivates them to collaborate, and how they interact, all of which are critical to determining how to gain business value from their interactions.

Growing communities is difficult. It will help if you can exploit existing online or real-world communities. A purpose roadmap will help determine whether to join an existing online community, move an offline community online, or form a new community. You can start with a well-defined purpose roadmap to catalyze a community, or examine an existing community to determine relevant current and future purposes. Purpose is critical either way.

A purpose roadmap provides a plan for how the community can deliver value over time and a basis for estimating necessary investments. A single purpose only gives a short-term view. But a purpose roadmap provides a much longer planning horizon.

People often ask us, "How can I change my company into one with a highly collaborative culture?" We respond by asking, "How do you eat an elephant?" You eat it one bite at a time. The same principle applies to community collaboration. You change culture a purpose at a time. Although you shouldn't choose a purpose that is counter to your culture, you can use a purpose roadmap to stretch culture over time.

Without a roadmap, you can only discuss business value in general terms—by saying, for example, that collaboration will "make us more productive," or "improve effective communications," or "increase knowledge sharing." Without a roadmap and its explicit goals, leaders will have trouble measuring success. A roadmap of well-defined purposes suggests specific goals that can be measured—for example, "use consultant networks to create more new business proposals," or "involve high-net-worth clients in the development of new financial products and services to increase their uptake."

A purpose roadmap allows you to grow a social media environment and ecosystem over time to address new purposes. Roadmaps provide the foundation for defining the system necessary to grow and expand the social media environment incrementally. They inform the design of the environment, including capabilities needed, structure, user experience, workflow assimilation, and system integration. Purpose roadmaps spawn project plans for augmenting the environment. In addition, they help you understand such organizational implications as legal issues, HR implications, cultural affinities and impediments, and compatibility with corporate policy.

A purpose roadmap can help you understand which people to tap when starting and growing the community, as well as what content is needed, when, to properly "seed" the system. When people join the community, they should see activity already under way and be able to derive immediate value from participating. If you don't have an explicit purpose for the community, you have no context for determining which content is appropriate for seeding or whom to court for early participation.

A purpose roadmap helps identify appropriate behaviors for the community. A compelling purpose roadmap makes clear what will be asked of community members and why they would continue to participate. Purpose does much to stave off bad or unproductive behaviors. It can focus participants on desired behaviors and alleviate the need for a long list of "don'ts" that can discourage participation. A good purpose will not eliminate entirely the need for additional policy regarding appropriate online conduct. A roadmap will help you plan for how policy, governance, and moderation requirements will need to change over time to accompany new purposes.

A prescriptive purpose roadmap is a plan, and it's essential for starting a community. But once up and running, the community itself will influence how the roadmap evolves. A thriving and productive community will surface its own purposes. These new purposes become part of the living roadmap. In chapter 9, we will describe how to assist the community in taking over its own destiny.

An Approach to Building Purpose Roadmaps

BlueCross® BlueShield® of Tennessee[2] (BCBST) built a purpose roadmap for one of the community opportunity statements—the Effective Use of Benefits community—that emerged from its preparation of an organizational vision.[3]

Engage members (customers), providers and BCBST to proactively collaborate around understanding and exercising benefits for more cost-effective member care to increase member satisfaction and retention, reduce BCBST customer support efforts, and inspire members to influence their employers/groups towards BCBST offerings.

Through brainstorming and analysis, BCBST planners defined ten purposes that represented how the community could remain engaged and deliver continuing value over time:

- *Shorten the benefits learning curve:* Existing and new members help each other understand and use benefits to enhance the value members receive from their benefits and to improve member retention.

- *Adapt to health-care reform:* Members and BCBST employees share information and concerns about health-care reform—how it will affect members' health care and health insurance—and about actions members can take to adapt to the new health care environment. This will improve member satisfaction and help BCBST adapt to the reforms.

- *Discover entitlements and discounts:* Members help each other find entitlements, freebies, and discounts that enhance their well-being, improve satisfaction, and increase member retention.

- *Share preventive health care:* Members and BCBST interact around the benefits of preventive care and such preventive actions as child immunizations, routine mammograms, and annual diabetes testing that improve members' health and well-being.

- *Find an ideal provider:* Members help each other find the right health-care providers (doctors, therapists, etc.) who are qualified, in-network, and available. They also can share experiences around how providers process benefits. This increases member satisfaction while improving BCBST's cost effectiveness and knowledge of service provided.

- *Prepare for life-changing events:* Members prepare for impending life events (retirement, marriage, children, etc.) by assisting each other in selecting an appropriate insurance plan. The goal is to ease the burden of changing plans and ensure proper insurance coverage.

- *Determine when and where to seek care:* Members assist one another in answering basic questions: "When do I need to seek care? Where should I go? Is this issue an emergency? If so, where do I go?" This improves member care and BCBST cost effectiveness.

- *Cut health-care red tape:* Members share experiences and successes in cutting health-care red tape and thus improving the service they receive. The goal is to increase member satisfaction and reduce the level of customer support BCBST must provide.

- *Deal with riders, limitations, and exclusions:* Members help one another understand how to interpret the limitations and exclusions (e.g., regarding birth-control pills, growth hormones) of the coverage provided by their employers. The goal is help members use that information, in conjunction with the policy itself, to proactively use their benefits. This will improve customer satisfaction and reduce the level of BCBST customer support required.

- *Control the cost of health care:* Members share tips on ways to control costs, exchange best practices for managing health care within plans, and help one another find and use BCBST benefits management tools.

Trevin Bernarding, Director of eBusiness Development at BCBST, stated that "Building purpose roadmaps really helped us shift our thought process, away from the social media technology, to a focus on how we should use it to deliver value to our members, our employees, and our business."[4] How did BCBST—and how do you—go about building purpose roadmaps? Develop a roadmap for each community by undertaking these activities:

1. Preparation

2. Defining the community

3. Brainstorming purposes

4. Evaluating and organizing purposes

5. Documenting the purpose roadmap

Preparation

To start, select a specific community from the Grow projects in your community collaboration portfolio and appoint a community sponsor, the individual who will lead the effort.

The sponsor then gathers the people who will draft a roadmap for the chosen community. Selecting the right people is critical. They should include representatives from the target community, others from the business units involved, and people from relevant support organizations, such as marketing, corporate communications, IT, legal, information security, and regulatory compliance.

Before this group meets, make all necessary logistical preparations and be sure to brief them adequately on the task before them.

Defining the Community

BCBST's Effective Use of Benefits opportunity statement broadly identified the target audience as members (insurance customers), health-care providers, and relevant BCBST staff. To develop a purpose roadmap, BCBST refined the audience further by identifying six key subgroups of participants:

- Small group/individual BCBST members

- Large group/employer members

- Government members

- BCBST customer service/consumer advisers

- BCBST care managers

- Health-care practitioners

As you define your community, combine subgroups if they share the same needs or provide the same benefits to a community. For example, if government-based members and large-group members in the BCBST list shared the same need for community collaboration and could offer similar value, there would be no need to list them separately.

Try to limit the list to six or fewer of the more important subgroups to keep the effort manageable and maintain a focus on top priority participants and interactions. For example, BCBST divided the members into small-group members (individuals), large-group members (employers), and government members. It also determined that customer service, consumer advisers, and care managers were the most important participants from BCBST staff. But customer service staff and consumer advisers were similar, and so they were combined into one subgroup. Finally, practitioners were considered the relevant provider subgroup.

Brainstorming Purposes

The goal of brainstorming purposes is to identify how community participants might collaborate in ways both meaningful to themselves and valuable to the organization. A purpose statement in a purpose roadmap takes the same basic form as the broader opportunity statements developed earlier in the vision stage. It says *who, collaborating around what, will benefit themselves and the organization in what ways?*

But the purpose statement must be more specific and personal. The target audience for the opportunity statements is the business whereas the audience for the purpose is composed of community participants. To see the difference, see table 6-1, which compares the opportunity statement for the BCBST community in our example with one of the more specific purpose statements brainstormed under it.

While the opportunity statement provides a good but broad business description of why a community should exist, it typically isn't specific or personal enough to be compelling to the participants it seeks to attract. The art of purpose brainstorming is in finding the level of specificity that will touch participants and motivate them to participate.

TABLE 6-1

Comparison of an opportunity statement and one of the purpose statements under it

Opportunity statement for the Effective Use of Benefits community	Purpose statement: "Preparing for life-changing events"
"Engage members, providers, and BCBST to proactively collaborate around understanding and exercising benefits for more cost-effective member care to increase member satisfaction and retention, reduce BCBST customer support efforts, and inspire members to influence their employers/groups toward BCBST offerings."	"Members prepare for impending life events (retirement, marriage, children, etc.) by assisting each other in selecting an appropriate insurance plan. The goal is to ease the burden of changing plans and ensure proper insurance coverage."

Purpose brainstorming is a creative endeavor because those involved must imagine new ways people might interact to improve their lives personally and deliver value to the organization. Two techniques can help you stimulate the flow of ideas:

- First, look at each of the subgroups you've identified (like the BCBST subgroups listed earlier) and for each ask these kinds of questions:

  - What are their goals in regard to the opportunity statement?

  - What is most important and meaningful to them?

  - What challenges do they face in regard to the opportunity statement?

  - How would members in this subgroup want to interact with each other? What can they learn from or teach each other?

- Second, look at how each subgroup might benefit from interacting and sharing information with others. For example, how might government members learn from or teach BCBST care managers? How might health-care practitioners learn from or teach small-group members? What goals and challenges do these groups share? How does BCBST want them to collaborate? Work your way systematically through all subgroups in this way.

Brainstorm somewhere between fifteen and twenty purpose statements, expecting that you will ultimately end up with around ten to twelve in the roadmap. Focus on highly compelling purposes that provide the most value to the organization and community.

Evaluating and Organizing Purposes

When you're done brainstorming purposes, you're ready to analyze them and then select and prioritize the dozen or so that will go into the roadmap. Validate and refine the purposes by checking that each is well defined, focused, and supports the opportunity statement for the overall collaborative community. If a purpose isn't community-driven, then recast or drop it. If it's too general to resonate with potential participants or so low-level that many won't find it meaningful, then discard it or recast it to overcome those deficiencies.

Next, evaluate and score the surviving purposes against the following five characteristics that every effective purpose should possess: magnetic, business aligned, low community risk, measurable, and facilitates evolution (these were described in detail in chapter 5).

Brainstorming teams often assign a value to each purpose for each of the five characteristics and record the rationale for each rating. Then they sum the five values for each purpose and sort the purposes from highest to lowest. With this prioritization and the rationales, they construct a draft roadmap for growing the community or establishing other social applications and communities.

An added benefit of the work in this step: the explanations of the ratings will provide critical information both for business justification and in launching the community collaboration environment.

Figure 6-2 shows a draft purpose roadmap developed by BCBST for the Effective Use of Benefits community. It depicts a plan for how the community can evolve over time to address more and more purposes, each flowing from the original opportunity statement.

FIGURE 6-2

BCBST purpose roadmap for the Effective Use of Benefits community

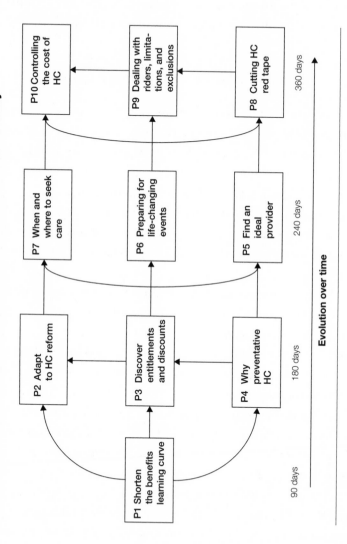

Documenting the Purpose Roadmap

Your draft of a roadmap will require further work. Show it to people in the target community and other key stakeholders for feedback. Incorporate any changes, prepare a final version, and add a timeline of when the various purposes in the roadmap will be pursued. (There's some possibility the next step—preparing a business justification for the community—will produce further modifications.) A complete roadmap should include:

- A purpose roadmap depicting the potential flow from one purpose to another, with a timeline. Though the timeline is only an estimate, especially for the medium and long term, it still can help with resource and effort planning

- A description of the target community and subgroups

- A description of each purpose

- The details of your analysis of each purpose, which can help in building the business justification and in guiding the community after launch

While there is still work to be done before launch, the roadmap is the core document defining the likely work of the community and the purposes it will pursue. Remember that the roadmap is a plan for possibilities, not a traditional project plan that's concrete and prescriptive. In a thriving community, member feedback and emergence will heavily influence the direction it takes.

Building a Business Rationale for a Collaborative Community

Earlier we explained the important role purpose roadmaps play in building the business justification for community collaboration efforts. Indeed, it is crucial. You can't build a business justification for collaboration in general. But you can and you should build one around specific business relevant purposes.

There is a surprising and destructive controversy under way in the press and on the social Web about whether business justification is appropriate for social media. It's a destructive discussion because building a business justification is indeed necessary, and it's hard work. If pundits give them the option, people will be more likely to take the easier path and forgo the work.

You need not do an extensive business justification or formal business case for every community. But you do have to explore and document fundamental questions about costs, benefits, risks, and, above all, business value. With grassroots efforts that got the green light, you've already explored costs and risks and found them minimal. A modest effort now at estimating business value for them can suffice. But recognize that justifying many community collaboration efforts will not be that easy. So the question is not whether you need to do a business justification but just how robust your business case needs to be.

Pursuing social media without a business justification is a mistake that is both pernicious and widespread. The practice of provide-and-pray, which contributes heavily to the high failure rate of social media initiatives, thrives in the absence of business justification. Failure to think about social media in terms of concrete business costs and benefits has led to disillusionment and raised questions in the C-suite about its organizational value.

Consequently, executives are interested in finding appropriate metrics and making the business case for social media. Organizations regularly ask for general social media return on investment (ROI) benchmarks. Unfortunately, there aren't any, at least none so far. Goals and results vary tremendously from purpose to purpose and from organization to organization. Much of this variation arises from inconsistencies in the ability of organizations to assess social media value. Some identify and realize clear benefits, while many do not.

A focus on business value begins with purpose because purpose is the basis for assessing value. Many organizations do seek and achieve definite returns on their investments in creating collaborative communities. While hard ROIs will be difficult to ascertain in many cases, business value analysis can and should be done.

Remember FICO from chapter 1? Their myFICO forums grew to over four hundred thousand registered members contributing more than ten thousand posts per month. Barry Paperno, Consumer Affairs Manager for myFICO.com, said, "With our myFICO social media forums we defined explicit business goals but purposely avoided hard ROI targets. We were able to grow a thriving community but when it came time to measure success it was, frankly, a bit scary. We didn't want to discover that this very active community wasn't actually delivering real business value." Oh, but it was. They found that people who participated in the forums had a 41 percent higher spend rate than myFICO.com customers who didn't. Thirty-nine percent of myFICO traffic was coming directly to the forums, and they were getting an 8 percent sales conversion rate. This number is significant considering that, intentionally, FICO doesn't promote products or engage in any sales and marketing activities within the forums. This conversion rate is purely community driven. Additionally, FICO experienced an 8 percent reduction in customer service calls that is directly attributed to the forums. Most posts are answered by other community members in less than seven minutes. All this combined gave FICO an ROI of greater than 300 percent. FICO achieved these results because they had a clear purpose for their forums and explicit business value goals.[5]

If the purposes you chose for a community don't show a path to tangible value, then choose different purposes until you find that path. Can substantial business value appear in the absence of a formal analysis and justification? Yes, but it will be accidental—and rare.

We often hear the argument: "Just do it. Social media tools are so cheap you don't need to build a business rationale based on costs and benefits." It's true that access to social media will often (though not always) be cheap; indeed, creating a corporate Twitter account or Facebook page is free. But how often will a corporate Facebook page do the job you want done?

Don't fall into this "It's cheap" trap. Launching a successful social media effort often has significant costs beyond the technology—costs around computing infrastructure, information security, administering and moderating the community, seeding, marketing to potential participants, integrating the environment with workflow practices and systems, change management, and productivity. And don't forget the cost of participation. People's time is not free. Significant success rarely, if ever, comes cheap or easy. Social media is no different.

In August 2009, the U.S. Marine Corps temporarily banned Marines from accessing the social Web until it could assess the costs and benefits and formulate a policy that minimized risk. The Corps reopened access in April 2010 after absorbing the costs of formulating, socializing, and enforcing that policy. At that point, network usage by Marines jumped so much the Corps had to increase its bandwidth, which was not cheap. Then, because Facebook is now the main source of threats to information security, the Marine Corps Recruiting Command had to install and maintain stronger security measures. All of this added up to significant costs—just for access to the social Web. Now the Marine Corps is seeking to apply social media more strategically to its mission. It anticipates investing even more, but it's proceeding with a clear eye on tangible costs and benefits.

If you've assembled a thoughtful purpose roadmap, you're well prepared for building the business justification. Defining purpose in terms of behaviors and measurable business value, as you will have done, provides the foundation for identifying tangible value and related costs. The more effort you invest in defining the purpose roadmap, the easier the business justification.

Building a Justification Story

To make the business case for a collaborative community, you must identify and capture the right pieces of information—we call them *elements*—and string them together to tell a complete end-to-end story (see figure 6-3).

FIGURE 6-3

Information elements needed to justify social media efforts

Traceability

1. Social principles	2. Social benefits	4. Business benefits	6. Business impact
Participation	Collective intelligence	Customer responsiveness	Revenue growth
Collective	Expertise location	Market responsiveness	Market share growth
Transparency	Emergent structures	Regulatory responsiveness	Better profitability
Independence	Interest cultivation	Sales effectiveness	Competitive position
Persistence	Mass coordination	Supplier effectiveness	Regulatory compliance
Emergence	Relationship leverage	Operational effectiveness	
	3. Social costs	Product development effectiveness	
	Architecture and design	Cost reduction or avoidance	
	Technology investment	**5. Business costs**	
	Seeding	Culture change	
	Promotion	Leadership participation	
	Participation	Process and system change	
	Administration and governance	Human capital	
	Information security	Business operations impact	
		Capital outlay	

The elements you need fall into six categories:

- Social principles (detailed in chapter 2)

- Social benefits (detailed in chapter 2)

- Social costs

- Business benefits

- Business costs

- Business impact

Organizations select the elements that are relevant to the specific community and link them to one another in order to create a coherent—*traceable*—story about how value is created.

Although FICO didn't use this method for their business justification, let's apply it to their myFICO forums to illustrate how this works:

- *Social benefits:* The purpose of the forums is to "Grow a community where people can help one another improve their credit score." The desire to improve and protect their credit rating is the main draw for the community, and so we know *interest cultivation* is a social benefit. And since people are looking to others for help, *expertise location* is another.

- *Business benefits:* The purpose also tells us that FICO is hoping the forums will provide an additional service to people in need and that some of their customers in the forums may drive others to purchase FICO products. So *market responsiveness* and *sales effectiveness* are target business benefits.

- *Business impact:* Given the business benefits identified— sales effectiveness and market responsiveness—*revenue growth* and *market share growth* are areas of business impact FICO will realize.

- *Social principles:* Now we return to the first box. Given the social benefits we've identified, it becomes clearer that the primary social principles at work here are *participation, collective, transparency,* and *emergence*. People collect and participate around the shared interest and through transparency expertise emerges. We can lay all this out as shown in figure 6-4. Traceability does not mean you must note all possible ties among elements. Include only the stronger elements and relationships, because they will provide a more compelling business justification.

- *Social and business costs:* What about the remaining categories of social costs and business costs? This narrowing of

FIGURE 6-4

myFICO forums business justification traceability chain

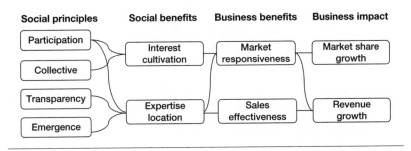

focus also provides the critical context for examining the costs associated with the social benefits (interest cultivation and expertise location) and business benefits (sales effectiveness and market responsiveness). For example, to generate interest FICO may need to seed the community with credit rating information and to court people who have significantly improved their credit scores as early adopters. Also, in order to gain additional benefits of increased market responsiveness, FICO may need to invest in social analytics technology and possibly increase their ability to analyze the community activity to deliver new or enhance existing products.

Combining the information elements, we have begun to show how social media can deliver business benefits by mobilizing a community around improving credit scores. We can flesh out this story by adding more detail about how the elements are linked and how each plays its role. Without purpose, there would be no story and therefore no tangible business justification.

In this chapter we focused on the two main aspects of refining the purpose of a community—a roadmap showing how a community can evolve to deliver sustained value over time and a justification describing the concrete sources of that expected value. This combination provides solid footing to progress to the launch phase, where a desired community becomes a reality.

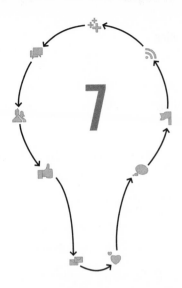

Launching the Community

Gartner Inc. is the world's largest information technology research and advisory firm with over sixty thousand clients in eleven thousand distinct organizations across the globe. Gartner recognized in social media a significant opportunity to serve its clients by fostering interaction among them around common IT challenges. Gartner believed a trusted collaborative environment populated with its content and facilitated by its analysts would be attractive to clients. Consequently, it created a collaborative environment called Peer Connect where clients could help each other answer difficult questions and gather around ongoing challenges. Gartner created a purpose roadmap for Peer Connect before progressing on to implementation.

Creating the purpose roadmap unearthed a set of critical questions that needed to be answered before the company could launch Peer Connect:

> With what client challenges should Gartner seed Peer Connect to attract participation? What initial groups should be formed around what important challenges?

How should employees interact in the environment? Should every group have an assigned facilitator? If so, how would the facilitators contribute?

How would Gartner manage client groups in Peer Connect to minimize duplication, inactivity, and otherwise keep them from becoming a chaotic mess?

What social media technologies would best support the purpose roadmap and how should they be sourced?

How should Gartner tie Peer Connect into existing company systems?

How should Gartner promote Peer Connect to its clients and get them actively engaged?

Nir Polonsky, Group Vice President of New Product Development, said, "As we examined purposes and participant experience, it became clear that making Peer Connect happen would involve much more than 'provide some technology.' So we took a very thoughtful and targeted approach to our launch efforts."[1]

Gartner moved through strategy and purpose roadmap efforts to arrive at a clear understanding of what it wanted from Peer Connect and the value it could provide participants. But it still faced the details of how to effectively deliver a collaboration environment that would actually attract participation and deliver that value.

The purpose roadmap answers many questions about why people will join and collaborate, but it also, as we see in the Peer Connect example, surfaces more questions about how they will collaborate. These questions capture the details, the mechanics, involved in collecting a community and facilitating purposeful collaboration. The launch stage is where you discover and deliver on these details.

This stage of our approach is about delivering a solution. It's about turning the purpose roadmap you created into reality. It's about creating the right social media environment and then attracting participants to it.

There are three key steps in launch:[2]

1. Exploring and defining the participant *experience*

2. Creating the right *environment*. Environment breaks down into three subactivities:

   – Creating *structure*

   – Delivering an *ecosystem*

   – Using the right *technologies*

3. *Engaging* the community. Engagement involves setting *critical mass targets* and rapidly driving participation to the *tipping point*.

These activities are best completed in a particular order. Figure 7-1 depicts an effective sequence.

If you've prepared properly and all goes well with the launch, you will then have people collecting into a community and collaborating around a shared purpose.

FIGURE 7-1

Flow of launch activities

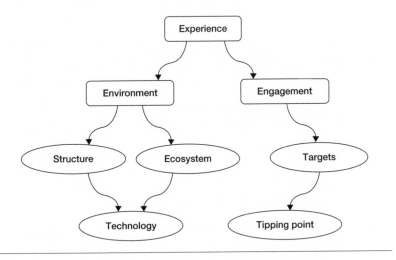

Explore the Participant Experience

A purpose roadmap says *why* people will take part in community collaboration. Participant experience deals with *how* people will collaborate and contribute. It's about the human experience of collaborating to achieve a purpose, not about the technology or interface. It's about making the collaboration experience productive and meaningful for community members. Exploring the experience involves examining and documenting specific actions community members will take when participating and how to support those behaviors.

The key to creating the right participant experience is to determine what participants want and value. Find out what is meaningful to them: Saving time? Feeling they are not alone? Doing better work? Getting the best result? Getting to a good outcome as quickly as possible? Support and counsel through a difficult situation? Feeling valued? For each purpose, list what is meaningful to participants and, based on that, define the core participant actions needed to realize that meaning.

Acosta, a leading North American sales, marketing, and service firm, recognized that Internet, social media, and mobile technologies were changing the in-store buying experience. Paul Price, Executive Vice President Marketing Services at Acosta, put it like this, "We know that social media is changing the shopper's experience. For proof of this, many of us need look no further than our own households. When my daughter shops for clothes she often will take a picture of herself wearing the item, post it on Facebook, and get her friend's opinions before deciding to buy."[3]

Indeed, before buying, many customers want to:

- Enlist the community of fellow customers and prospects in finding the product right for them

- Determine easily if the price is right

- Understand others' experiences with the product and be able to contribute their experiences to the community

- Know if the company producing the product is socially responsible

This is what's important to them, and, if they can't get this information in the store, then they won't shop or buy there. Acosta knows that the "store of the future" must recognize and address these buyer values. Knowing these, Acosta can walk through the collaborative buying experience customers want and identify actions they will want to take. Thus, Acosta knows a store of the future must allow customers to:

- Determine before going to a store nearby if it carries a product and if it's in stock

- Locate a product once they're in the store

- Engage with the community of customers and prospective buyers while in the store to make a buying decision

- Get basic social feedback on the product, in addition to product information and pricing, at the shelf

- Quickly and easily access more detailed product information at the shelf

- Gain access at the shelf to custom sale pricing and group promotions, or coupons

- Share their product opinions and buying decisions with others in the store

This kind of information is critical to the design of the social media environment. It reflects the need to blend the online and offline experience with multiple touch points, including store, kiosk, shelf, Web, and mobile. It also may require combining social media with other technologies, such as context awareness and business intelligence. Paul Price remarked that, "Exploring possible social media impacts on the shopper's experience encouraged us to step back and reexamine the whole shopper path to purchase."[4]

Exploring the participant experience (of in-store shoppers in this case) can provide a more holistic view of buyers' needs and the social experience of in-store shopping. In sum, look at the collaboration experience you're creating through the lens of participants' needs and values. Design the experience to satisfy them. If you don't, you reduce the chances of adoption.

In addition to exploring a purpose-specific experience, there are a set of more general user experience techniques and approaches that are gaining popularity in social media environment design. A few worth noting are design thinking, empathy maps, and gamification. The first two are methodologies for connecting with users to deliver a meaningful experience. Gamification is the application of game theory and mechanics to non-game activities. In social media, gamification often takes the form of granting points or virtual currency for valuable contributions. As people accumulate points or currency they gain social status in the community. This status is normally reflected in titles, badges, and leader boards representing level progression. The level progression may include additional capabilities in the social media environment.

Create a Community Collaboration Environment

Gartner's Peer Connect project faced some fundamental challenges in designing the collaborative environment. The purpose roadmap, plus Gartner's efforts to understand participants' experience in the environment, revealed particular requirements for the collaborative environment. In other words, what structures must the environment offer to encourage and facilitate participation? Free-form collaboration doesn't mean a blank slate. The environment should guide participants and make contributing as easy as possible.

An online collaborative environment needs not only content but also ways to access that content and to create new content, mechanisms for organizing and valuing content and contributors, guidelines for participation, and some level of community administration.

To design and deliver such an environment successfully, you must satisfy certain fundamental requirements:

- The environment must have the right amount of structure to facilitate productive participation without stifling creativity.

- The environment must be simple, with a learning curve that requires no more than two minutes.

- The environment needs to be integrated into participants' broader ecosystems. It can't be separate or isolated from the way people normally work, play, buy, and so on.

- Participants must be able to quickly and effortlessly find what they need from the often voluminous mass of community contributions.

- Participants must see clear and compelling value immediately upon entering the environment.

- The technology must be chosen carefully so that it facilitates participation while seeming invisible.

Delivering the Right Amount of Structure

A collaborative environment requires some structure, including functionality, user interface design, authoring templates, tagging structures, content templates, place configuration (e.g., virtual worlds), and workflow. There is much talk around social media of unstructured and free-form collaboration. But a lack of structure can be risky and create problems that stifle adoption.

Too little structure can be as limiting as too much. Without structure, participants receive little guidance and find it difficult to be productive. Too much structure, on the other hand, can create steep learning curves and impede emergence. You must find the right balance. As always, the key is to create just enough structure.

For example, one firm wanted to collect and share stories from employees who dealt directly with clients. It asked the employees to record with their stories such client information as company size, location, product type, and so on. However, employees in different roles would find different characteristics relevant. So the firm thought about allowing employees to choose the characteristics they considered most important. Each employee-defined characteristic would become a new field in the database, and other employees would have access to these fields and either use them or add their own. This way, rather than provide a predefined information structure, the "right" data structures would emerge through community use.

However, the purpose of the effort was to capture client stories, not create an emergent database through community-defined fields. The effort involved in finding the right community-determined characteristics or defining new ones would, in fact, detract from the main goal of collecting stories. Moreover, the potential for a large and messy database containing information across employee-defined fields would be antithetical to the goal of "collecting" information. In the end, the organization provided a small number of generally defined fields where participants could add whatever text they felt relevant. In this situation, it would have been counterproductive to leave the database unstructured and allow a socially built structure to emerge. Providing some guidance in advance both supported the purpose and allowed people to be more productive right from the start.

But resist the urge to overengineer. Provide the minimal structure required to make participation productive. Whatever level of structure you choose, it should:

- Promote achievement of the purpose

- Minimize the participant learning curve

- Guide productive behaviors

- Deliver perceived value

- Encourage emergence directly relevant to the purpose

More structure generally means more bells and whistles, which leads to a more complicated environment and a steeper learning curve. If you must choose between more structure and ease of use, choose ease of use.

Ease of Use Is Paramount

Ease of use is the mantra for all IT applications, but for social media, where contribution is always completely voluntary, it's absolutely vital. You simply can't force good collaboration. Nonetheless, many organizations lose sight of this fact and instead add more bells and whistles in hopes of attracting more participants. In social media, however, less really is more because bells and whistles don't attract a community—a compelling purpose does.

The most successful collaborative communities start out small in scope and large in scale. They have a powerfully attractive, tightly defined purpose (supported by a highly integrated purpose roadmap) that appeals to a large number of people. One highly magnetic purpose is always better than three of lesser appeal. The more purposes in the launch, the broader the scope. The broader the scope, the greater the functionality (bells and whistles) needed. The greater the functionality, the steeper the learning curve. The steeper the learning curve, the bigger the obstacle to adoption. Hence, a wide array of appealing purposes at one time can actually impede mass adoption. Because community collaboration depends on growing the community to critical mass, adoption is the number-one goal.

Google was certainly not the first Internet search engine, but it was the easiest to use. Google rapidly surpassed the competition with a single text box in the middle of a mostly blank page. It could not have been simpler.

The Google approach of "less is more," where substantial power lies behind a simple interface, should be the primary design consideration for all social media. If a social media environment requires training, it will fail. How many people are Facebook-certified? Who has gone to a Wikipedia class or attended Craigslist workshops? These environments manage to attract hundreds of millions of participants without a single minute of training. The major successes on the social Web don't need to train their users, and neither should organizations.

If you have achieved the right amount of structure without sacrificing ease of use, then the environment will encourage content contribution. This can cause a massive influx of content—a good thing, assuming you're prepared for it. If you're not, this "good thing" will clog your collaboration environment and render it unusable.

Delivering an Ecosystem

Social media is a consumerization phenomenon. It started and grew from consumer behavior on the public Web and is now influencing organizations. As a result, many employees are going outside their organization's IT systems and turning to the public Web and cloud computing for their social software needs.

This can create numerous *social islands*—collaborative spaces on the public Web that serve, often effectively, the needs of relatively small groups such as teams or business units. The problem is that these spaces are isolated from the rest of the organization, which limits their value to the organization as a whole while creating problems around data duplication, data security, governance, duplication of effort, manual processing, and disjointed workflows.

The isolation also curtails the value of social islands as true mass collaboration environments because participation is artificially limited to the originating suborganization. This weakness applies as well to isolated and disjointed market-facing social media efforts. This is not a matter of in-house or on-premises versus third party or social Web environments; it's a matter of connectedness. Rather than having employees default to the social Web, you should decide on the best place to put your environment for collaboration and, wherever it's located, tie it into existing interconnected systems and practices, the ecosystem, as needed.

You connect your collaboration environment in your organization's ecosystem by tying it into existing communication, collaboration, organization search, knowledge-management, and content-management systems. For example, with Peer Connect, Gartner wanted to apply the power of its research-based content when clients posed a question in the environment. This meant Peer Connect had to be integrated to some extent with Gartner's content-publishing system.

For market-facing social media efforts, the effort might mean linking the environment to sales, marketing, and customer management systems and processes. For social media aimed at employees, it could mean tying the environment to operational systems and processes. Participation may drop drastically if users must manually move information between the social media environment and workplace systems.

Integrating social media into existing systems in this way can make organizational environments for collaboration much more attractive to employees than their self-selected and isolated public Web environments.

Making Information Easily Discoverable

In social media, everyone can be a creator of content. That's why the amount of content on the public Web is exploding, and now it's exploding for organizations too. The result is content overload that demands new and more comprehensive ways to find information. Nobody wants to slog through a mass of irrelevant contributions.

Easy discoverability is a key component of creating a good user experience. Other alternatives, such as folder and directory navigation, don't work well with huge volumes of information or deliver a good participant experience.

A robust enterprise search capability is mandatory, but it isn't enough. Google convinced everyone that surfing is bad and searching is good. However, a poor search result can cause superficial surfing between the search engine and the resulting links.

You need to take a more holistic approach, which can be summarized in the *five S's* of information discoverability.

- *Search:* Enterprise search, where a broad body of content is indexed for fast retrieval, lets participants view a set of results that may address their needs or provide an entry point for further discovery.

- *Subset:* Subset is the ability to organize or reduce voluminous search results through capabilities like sorting, suggestions, and filtering.

- *Surf:* Surfing is the discovery of information by traversing meaningful content links. Wikipedia is a good example. People use a search engine to find an entry point into it and then surf via embedded links from article to article.

- *Social:* Community (social) feedback can improve the ability to find relevant information. Social feedback technologies—such as rating, ranking, voting, investing, commentary, badging, and tagging—can add substantial value. The community decides what information is most useful, how it's useful, and how it relates to other content. In this way, the most useful information, as determined by the community, floats to the top.

- *Subscribe:* Subscription technology such as RSS (really simple syndication) helps participants designate the specific information they want most, and then they're notified when new material is available, or they have it sent (pushed) to them automatically.

Without this more holistic approach to information validation and discovery, the fruit of your highly engaged and wildly prolific community may turn into a mostly unusable mess.

Seeding the System for Immediate Participant Value

Participants will not find value in an empty social media environment. And most will be impatient even when an environment is brand-new. So you must give users, from the beginning, a reason to visit and contribute. Seed the system with initial content and key participants consistent with the community's purpose and business goals. Another benefit of seeding is that it can help facilitate any efforts to integrate the community with existing systems to deliver a flow of content. However, seeding can quickly become costly and time-consuming. Examine the need for it carefully and take into account these considerations:

- What content is required to show immediate value to new community members?

- What constitutes valuable "purpose supporting" content that can be readily migrated or integrated?

- What key people or roles need to participate up front to add credibility and value to the environment?

- What integration with existing systems will participants expect initially?

- What content will help participants contribute their own content?

- How will seeding affect implementation costs and schedules?

The collaborative environment must contain enough base content and initial participation to provide new participants with immediate and recognizable value, encourage them to contribution actively, and lead them to invite their colleagues, friends, and others. For example, Gartner understood that gaining active and productive participation is always a challenge. So they explicitly defined the desired collaborative behaviors to determine the specific functionality, content, and other mechanisms that would motivate participants to engage in valuable discussions.

Selecting the Right Social Media Technology

Choosing the right social media technology can be a challenge because so much variety is available. The key options occur mostly in functionality, sourcing alternatives, and customization.

Functionality. Social media technologies offer a vast range of capabilities. Even general social media such as social networking,

FIGURE 7-2

Social technology capabilities

General	Specialized	Supporting
Social networking	Idea engine	Alerts
Wikis	Prediction market	Tagging, badging
Blogs	Crowdsourcing	Social analytics
Microblogs	Answer marketplace	Subscriptions
Threaded discussions	Web reputation	Social status
Social feedback	Viral campaign	Mobile
Social publishing	Social learning	Context aware

wikis, and blogs vary significantly and work best for different uses. Figure 7-2 lists the primary social media capabilities currently available.

It's easy to make the wrong choice. Even buying a general-purpose social technology suite (an integrated set of social functions) may not offer the capability you really need. Every suite has strengths and weaknesses, even in core capability.

Applying the wrong technology can undermine success. For example, using a wiki to gather, augment, and vet ideas will fail, even on a moderate scale. Wikis don't allow the community to perform those activities in a systematic manner so that the best ideas float to the top and incomplete, duplicative, irrelevant, or unpopular ideas fall from sight. At the time of writing over one hundred thousand ideas have been submitted to Starbucks at http://mystarbucksidea.force.com. Imagine dealing with that volume in an environment like Wikipedia. Wikis can produce a quagmire of content where the value of one idea is indistinguishable from another. This isn't a criticism of wikis. Wikis are intended for dynamic, unbounded, multi-author documentation, not idea management. Scalable idea management requires specialized social technology.

Sourcing Options. As with technology, there are many social technology sources from which you can choose. As you think about sourcing, ask three important questions.

1. *Should you build your own social community or join an existing social Web community such as Facebook, LinkedIn, or PatientsLikeMe.com?* Social media adds a third option—join—to the traditional choice of "buy versus build." There are hundreds of existing social communities on the Web, from general sites such as Facebook, YouTube, and Wikipedia to specific sites like PatientsLikeMe.com (for those with illnesses), fliesandfins.com (for fishing aficionados), and Livemocha.com (for learning a new language). Why build your own social community if you can achieve your purpose on someone else's?

2. *Do you want an on-premise technology or a cloud computing–based service offering?* Many organizations considering social media don't possess a core competence in building world-class, highly scalable, social media infrastructure. Does it make more sense to grow that capability in-house or find a cloud computing provider of social media software as a service (SaaS)?

3. *Do you want software, or do you want a solution? If a solution, how full-service does the solution need to be?* Is it software you need or something more? Different vendors offer varying capabilities to support their software. Some provide basic technical support while others offer a full-service experience—from strategy and design to implementation, community formation, administration, and content management and moderating.

Customization. How much customization are you willing to endure? Every approach to developing the necessary technical capabilities has its advantages, disadvantages, and costs. However, three basic strategies for choosing a social media technology are emerging:

- The most adventuresome strategy, usually taken by leading-edge organizations that hope to gain competitive advantage through social media, is the *best-of-breed* approach in which they choose the best or most suitable technology in each category of social media tools. These organizations are willing to spend the time and resources needed to integrate these disparate tools into a coherent custom technology suite. Such firms typically already possess strong IT capabilities.

- A less aggressive approach is usually taken by progressive firms that feel they can achieve significant gains from social media or believe it's a competitive necessity. They choose a *commercial off-the-shelf* (COTS) general-purpose social software suite such as Jive Software, SocialText, or Drupal. They're willing to augment the COTS suite with point tools for more specialized social functionality, such as idea engines and answer marketplaces.

- More conservative organizations tend to build on their *existing content management* (ECM) technologies with social point tools. They are content to wait while their ECM vendor's product evolves before adding social capabilities to their platforms.

How to Choose? The task of choosing social media technology can be daunting. If you don't know your purpose, your chance of selecting the right social technology is just that—a chance. But with a solid understanding of purpose, the choice of technology is relatively straightforward. Purpose enables a deeper examination of participant experience, seeding requirements, systems integration, content discovery, and so on, all of which contribute critical information for a careful choice of the social technology needed to support it all. You can make the technology decision first and force community collaboration into that box. Or you can understand community collaboration first and choose suitable technology. Which do you think is the better approach for gaining adoption? Which do you think is the more prevalent approach? Unfortunately, while understanding first is better by far, choosing technology first is far more common.

Engage the Community

Once you've chosen the right social media technology and created a great participant experience around a compelling purpose, only one question remains. Will they come? Maybe not. You still need to grab and hold participants' attention. If they don't know the community exists or don't feel compelled to investigate it or don't find anything of interest when they do, they won't congregate. You need to engage them.

At one time, MySpace was the world's dominant social network. It pioneered the new world of mass collaboration and attracted millions of members. Many people believe its success occurred spontaneously just because it put a cool technology on the Web and people flocked to it in droves.

In fact, that's not true. MySpace took key traditional marketing steps specifically intended to drive membership. It started with a contest among employees of its parent company at the time, Intermix, offering a cash award to whoever signed up the most friends. It capitalized on the 100 million–plus names in its e-mail database. These steps brought some success but not enough for critical mass. Then MySpace noticed that the site was attracting music aficionados, and began courting bands, promoters, and clubs in Los Angeles with more traditional (that is, offline) marketing activities. Membership began growing more rapidly. Finally, it attracted people by leveraging its existing marketing relationships with some of the stronger Internet properties.[5] Only then did it hit the tipping point where contagious growth took over. Like the vast majority of social media successes, hard, proactive work was required to engage the community and reach the tipping point.

The vast majority of unsuccessful social media efforts fail for lack of adoption—people don't come at all, they don't come back, or they don't actively contribute. A compelling purpose is crucial, but it won't do the engagement work for you. To achieve critical mass you must first define it. Then you must engage the community and drive it to the tipping point.

Setting Critical Mass Targets

The success of a collaborative community will depend on attracting participant contributions. In the most successful social media environments, the vast majority of content comes from the community, not the organization. Everyone in the target community is a potential author. It's up to you, the organization, to entice participants to contribute.

Obviously, not every member will contribute. How many contributors do you need? What percentage of originators, augmenters (those who respond in some way to original contributions), and readers will lead to a productive and effective community? The 1-9-90 rule (or "1 percent rule") says that for every 100 participants, there will be 1 originator, 9 augmenters, and 90 readers.[6]

The 1 percent rule comes from experience on the social Web. Since the general public is the target community there, the 1 percent rule won't apply to all communities. For example, a community with a purpose targeted at employee engineers might require a very different participation ratio. A family using the social Web to keep each other up to date by sharing photos, messages, and videos will also experience a different ratio.

You should determine the level of community participation required for each collaborative community to reach critical mass. This participation target, which will vary for each community, can serve as an overall goal and provide a means to assess adoption success.

For example, consider an organization that wishes to create a community where its salespeople can collaborate around overcoming buyer objections. It might decide it needs a ratio of 10-40-50 per month to achieve critical mass and a self-sustaining community. Applying this ratio to the target audience of one thousand salespeople says there should be one hundred salespeople who originate content every month—say, a question about how to overcome a particular objection—and four hundred people who respond by offering an answer to the question. The remaining five hundred salespeople will simply read what's been posted. Of course, which salespeople contribute, augment, and simply read will change month to month, so that over time all or most all salespeople will participate.

Community contributions are certainly critical, but participation by those who only read others' content is also important and should not be undervalued. Reading by itself provides many of the benefits of collaborative communities. Members can learn, for example, how to handle an objection simply by reading the points raised and discussed by others. Here we see the power of a community. It amplifies the knowledge of each individual member—knowing how to handle a particular objection, for example—by making it available to the whole community. A solution to a problem, an innovative idea, an astute observation that would otherwise be lost gains enormous value when the masses can seize and act on it.

The targets you set for critical mass are estimates based on knowledge of the community, its purpose, and the estimated level of activity required for healthy community collaboration. Though they're estimates, such targets are important. They serve as a goal for motivating people to participate in a community, and so your marketing efforts should be directed at achieving them. They will influence how much you promote the community, as well as how you promote it and to whom. They will help establish the extent of the marketing effort, including resources and timing to reach the level of participation where the community will take on a life of its own and sustain itself.

Getting the Community to the Tipping Point

Social media environments do not grow slowly over time. They may die slowly, but that's not how they reach critical mass. Our research has shown that participants who find a community interesting will investigate to see if it offers any value. If there's no activity, they won't participate. When asked if they would return to the community site a second time if offered the right enticements, about 30 percent said they would. However, fewer than 1 percent said they would return a third time if, on the second visit, they still found no activity and nothing of value. Potential participants tend to be impatient and unforgiving in their assessment of collaborative communities. With community collaboration, momentum matters.

Community collaboration grows in a tipping-point fashion (see figure 7-3 below). You must create and execute on a tipping-point

FIGURE 7-3

The community tipping point

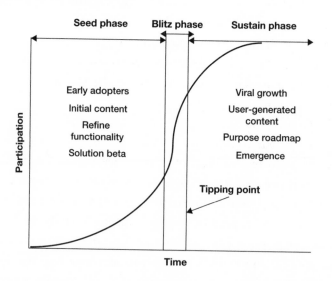

Source: Anthony J. Bradley, "Ten Primary Design Considerations for Delivering Social Software Solutions: The PLANT SEEDS Framework," Gartner Inc., July 13, 2009.

plan to reach critical mass as quickly as possible. A good tipping-point plan has three phases: seed, blitz, and sustain.

- *Seed phase:* Here you place initial content in the environment and court early adopters, sometimes by name. The seed phase offers organizations an opportunity to collect initial feedback and make refinements. Avoid proofs of concept, prototyping, piloting, or testing on the community. As we said, potential participants are unforgiving, and you may only get one shot at catalyzing a collaborative community. Try out the tools as much as you want in the laboratory, but don't go to the community until you can go with the full intention of succeeding, not for further testing. Proceed with all the discipline of any important project implementation. While pilots and prototypes may reduce risk and allow for further refinement, you can achieve the same outcomes with a tightly defined purpose and a properly executed seed phase.

- *Blitz phase:* In keeping with its name, the blitz phase is short but powerful. Before and during the seed phase, you should begin preparing for a blitz marketing campaign. When the seed phase reaches a predetermined level of readiness and activity, execute the blitz campaign, which is aimed at driving as much traffic to the community as quickly as possible, promoting viral membership, and achieving critical mass. The targets you set earlier for critical mass will serve as your tipping-point goal.

- *Sustain phase:* As a community approaches critical mass and viral growth drives more traffic, you can reduce your marketing efforts. In the sustain phase, your efforts should be aimed at achieving self-sustaining growth and emergence. Although the organization should maintain a purpose roadmap for facilitated growth, the now-active community can direct its own development so long as it doesn't evolve in a way that compromises value to the organization.

A growing best practice is to link the tipping-point plan around a major external event. Electronic Arts used the launch of new game titles to drive traffic to those of its communities that were tied to specific products. If no suitable external event is available, you might include a sponsored physical event as part of the blitz marketing campaign. The goal of the event is to grab attention and use that to gain membership and to inspire conversations and interactions within the team. Electronic Arts also held physical, conference-style meetings to kick off certain employee communities. It held discussions around the community's purposes and positioned the community collaboration environment as the ongoing venue for continuing progress.

The purpose of the tipping-point plan is to make sure visitors have a reason to return, contribute, and recruit new members. That reason hinges on community activity. In his book, *The Tipping Point*, Malcolm Gladwell describes different types of people who are relevant to moving ideas to the tipping point. Among them are *connectors* (those who know everybody) and *mavens* (those who know everything).[7] Identify and court both types early so that when the masses come to the environment they see *existing* valuable participation. An empty technology environment won't inspire anyone to contribute.

Once you get the community to the tipping point and it achieves critical mass, it will start taking on a life of its own. When this occurs, you and the organization will need to fundamentally shift your relationship with the community. It takes disciplined effort and control to drive a community to critical mass, but when that's achieved the community will take control of its own destiny. At this point, the organization must let go and guide.

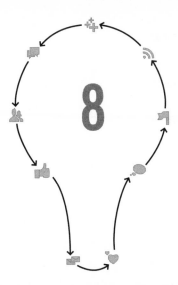

Guiding from the Middle

Electronic Arts (EA) launched internal collaborative communities in 2008 across its globally distributed workforce. Its goal was to gain the efficiencies of a large enterprise without compromising local teams' autonomy or creativity. The concept was based on an analogy described by EA's CEO, John Riccitiello, that was used to communicate EA's transformation to a new social organization as the difference between a swim meet and water polo match. At a swim meet, each group competes by having its swimmers compete individually in different events and by swimming in their own lanes with little interaction between teammates. A water polo match, on the other hand, features two teams, each comprised of individuals working together by collaboratively passing the ball to score goals.[1]

The initial interest in EA's launch of internal communities was strong, as many employees wanted to see how this new organizational concept would help them better connect, share, and collaborate. But EA initially launched too many communities, too quickly. Multiple communities diluted participation, which caused people to conclude the approach was ineffective, and the participation in some communities waned. "We launched with fifteen communities, but we soon found that in order to have a viable community you need at minimum thirty to fifty active participants. We should have targeted between four and six communities instead," said Michael Cuthrell, Director, Global IT. "That way we could have worked with the initial pilot communities to see which techniques and incentives spurred the most participation and carried over those successes to future communities."

Since the communities were launched in an enterprise setting, EA introduced a light governance model to manage and operate their communities, because too much structure would defeat the purpose of promoting the organic interaction and collaboration (and too little structure would have left the communities becoming little more than people with like-minded interests coming together to just talk). With that, EA settled on a three-tiered structure—an overall community steering committee, a competency center, and the actual communities themselves—and had defined processes and tools to support the communities. But the company found it needed more than structure: it needed a certain amount of active management to channel the organization's energy into productive communities and results. With this guidance, the communities transformed into a focused set of groups that now engages 75 percent of the IT organization—20 percent being highly active—in making connections across the enterprise, sharing ideas, and collaborating to make decisions. The communities were achieving what EA wanted—the benefits of scale without compromising the independence and creativity that makes EA unique.

EA's experience also makes clear the need for management to support mass collaboration—management not in the sense of controlling but in the spirit of working within the community to help members refine their purpose as well as to motivate participation, generate a flow of ideas, and facilitate decisions should the community become deadlocked. The community competency center works with communities to increase their participation and improve their tools and templates. Community sponsors represent each community and its decisions in the broader organization. The

EA story highlights an essential ingredient in becoming a social organization—the need to combine management guidance with mass collaboration.

After you launch a community, assuming all goes well, its members coalesce around a compelling purpose and freely volunteer their experience, knowledge, and ideas. Without formal hierarchy or imposed leadership beyond a sponsor and a few early adopters, the community evolves its own way of working and makes decisions based on its specific purpose and the collective needs and desires of its members.

This way of working is captured in the collaboration cycle that communities follow and that we first described in chapter 2 (see figure 8-1).

The cycle shows how a community's purpose elicits members' contributions, which receive feedback from other members in the

FIGURE 8-1

How collaborative communities do their work

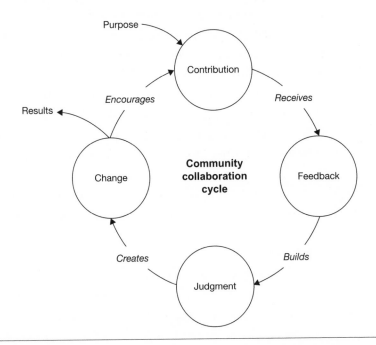

form of comments, related ideas, expansions of the original contributions, disagreement, questions, and so on. From the feedback emerges some form of community judgment about the value or status of the various ideas and proposals put forth and discussed. As a few ideas, directions, or decisions emerge and rise to prominence, they create new behaviors and change.

Here is the question you must now answer: *What is the role of management in this process?*

Many social media advocates are likely to say the role of managers is simple—do nothing. They think managers only get in the way of collaboration, creativity, and contribution. Without freedom to pursue its purpose on its own, they claim, a community cannot become truly collaborative. And, if it's not collaborative, it won't elicit the best thinking, ideas, efforts, and willingness to share of its members.

We disagree, having learned otherwise from our observations of successful communities in action. We acknowledge the clear dangers of too much management or the wrong kind of management. But for us the real question is not whether managers should get involved but how they should get involved *in the right way*.

Managers need to be involved, first, because they retain responsibility for results and, second, because every group needs some structure and guidance to be productive. Every group, whether a nation or a doubles tennis team, contains forces that pushes members together—such as a common purpose—as well as forces that pull them apart, such as disagreement that turns personal, cultural differences, and a dozen other forces that flow from the complexities and paradoxes of human nature.

Thus, the answer to the question "What is the role of management?" is not, "No role." But it's also not the role managers traditionally play.

Some structure and guidance is clearly needed, but how much? Just enough will help create an environment where individuals participate, become a community, and collaborate to create value. But too much will stifle or destroy collaboration because of one simple immovable fact: you cannot compel someone to participate or to share knowledge, experience, and ideas. Collaborative communities, by definition, are voluntary. If they're not, they're not collaborative.

Because of this fact, managers responsible cannot rely on their formal authority and the fear of consequences to produce the results they want. In collaborative communities, authority plays only a small role and the fear of consequences almost none at all.

Given these truths and what we've seen managers do in successful collaborative communities, we believe there are three key roles you as a manager must play:

- First, you must ensure that the collaboration cycle (figure 8-1) works productively, that the community is able to find its way through all the steps without obstruction and undue friction. This means you must guide—not direct or control—to the extent the purpose requires, which can mean:

  - For workforce-based, top-down community collaboration efforts, achieving the purpose may demand direct participation of the manager as a member.

  - Grassroots community managers must at least observe and respond, if necessary, to keep the community moving in the right direction.

  - Externally facing communities require managers who observe and refine policy and functionality in order to promote productive behaviors and facilitate a healthy collaboration cycle.

Because your primary aim here is to foster extensive contributions and feedback by individual members, we call this role *participation.*

- Second, you must keep the community productively focused on and moving toward its purpose. This involves actively monitoring progress against the purpose. This is how you ensure that the community creates value for the organization. This may even, in certain circumstances, require you to step in and refocus or restructure the community to achieve its purpose. This role, of course, we label *purpose.*

- Third, you must represent the collaborative community in the context of the organization as a whole. Here you pursue two aims: the first is to ensure that organizational systems, functions, and processes support rather than stifle the work of collaborative communities. The second is to create and sustain those links between your community and the organization that allow solutions and innovations generated by the community to flow throughout the organization and improve its overall performance. Without such links, the benefits of collaboration will be limited and remain locked up within the community that created them. This third role we call *performance.*

Participation. Purpose. Performance. These are the goals of management in its work with the individuals, communities, and organization engaged in mass collaboration. In the remainder of this chapter, we will focus on your role as manager in fostering the participation of community members. In the following two chapters, we will discuss purpose and performance in detail.

What Does "Guiding from the Middle" Mean?

Guiding is a useful way to think about the manager's role in a collaborative community. A guide is knowledgeable about the territory and provides advice about direction, distance, conditions, and alternate routes. A guide arranges or provides necessary resources and makes special arrangements when the group enters unfamiliar territory. A guide makes decisions, but only when asked or when the group is in danger. Guiding from the middle blends approaches for leading from the front and supporting from behind. Guiding requires employing a spectrum of techniques from obvious direct involvement to silent and steady advocacy.

Guidance by sponsors and managers starts with how managers handle the critical transition from pre- to post launch. The inability of managers to change the way they engage and evolve a community is one of the primary reasons social media initiatives fail. Our examination of hundreds of social media initiatives in a wide range of companies has identified the following challenges that managers must confront and resolve in this crucial shift from preparation to letting go:

- Letting go of ownership and shifting it to the community itself

- Encouraging the emergent nature of communities

- Keeping the community connected to the organization

- Creating transparency by providing information and maintaining visibility across the community

These practices describe how managers get involved in mass collaboration in ways that produce results without restraining the capacity of the community to create value.

Shift Ownership to the Community Itself

Throughout the purpose and launch stages, sponsors and managers exercise significant control in planning and setting up the community. They champion the community, identify opportunities, create the purpose roadmap, and advocate for the community in the organization. But once the community achieves the critical mass that marks the end of launch and the start of the guide stage, the role of managers must change.

Ownership of the work—decisions about what to do and how to do it—must belong to the community. Unless a group of people with a shared interest can act autonomously, they cannot form a true community and become or remain self-sustaining. This places two requirements on managers: (1) that they allow control to rest in the hands of the community itself; and (2) that they create a supportive organizational framework within which the community can form and do its work.

Shifting ownership is an important first step because an absence of interference allows members to build a community as the tipping-point plan drives participants to the collaboration site. Indeed, managers encourage this by limiting their own direct participation in early community discussions. This doesn't mean they should ignore these important discussions, but they should simply listen to understand how community members see the purpose, its value, and the immediate issues that need to be addressed. In some cases, sponsors and managers at this stage may need to step in to provide guidance, but only if the community is having trouble forming or if the purpose is going astray.

Direct participation in externally facing communities is often not possible. In these situations, management guides the community by seeding new interactions and purposes, rewarding different behaviors, and adjusting community policy and how it's enforced. Reserve these actions for situations in which things are going very wrong. Avoid drastic action by recognizing that externally facing communities need time to establish themselves.

This can be particularly difficult when the community purpose concerns specific operational or technical issues. Managers responsible for results will be eager for the community to "get to work." They must give the community a chance to form and find itself. Managers at CEMEX, for example, point out that it took some time for their communities to coalesce, but once they did, they typically developed a comprehensive and sophisticated view of the issues.

Allow the Community to Evolve to Achieve Its Purpose

A community needs to feel responsible for achieving its purpose. Unlike the way organizations traditionally work, responsibility cannot be assigned to a community because a community will accept responsibility only if it's free to determine its own course. That means it may modify its purpose, revise its roadmap, resequence priorities, redefine key issues, or require new tools—all of which will call for great latitude from management. The alternative, telling people what to do while discouraging any deviation from plan, will drain energy and creativity from a collaborative community, stifle participation, and ultimately drive members away.

As a manager, you will find this situation personally challenging. Supporting self-determination and evolution is difficult when you've advocated and directed preparations for the community. Most likely, you feel responsible for it—in fact, you may actually bear personal responsibility for its results. But it's like working with a high-potential employee: you must give each community the support and resources it needs to act and the guidance necessary to protect it, but you cannot direct what it does or how it proceeds.

If this is a workforce-based community, you can carefully begin to participate as it evolves its practices and approaches by asking neutrally phrased penetrating questions that raise important issues and focus attention without prejudicing the answers; for example, such simple but powerful questions as: "How does this contribute to the purpose?" "What are the implications of this for such-and-so?" "Why is this the best way to pursue the purpose at this time?" "What if such-and-so happens?" You also can praise current practices and progress. Management involvement helps the community evolve, gain understanding, and carry out its purpose. It also shows management interest in the community and, if done correctly, can motivate participation.

Participate in the Collaborative Cycle

To guide from the middle, sponsors and managers must take responsibility for promoting productive participation in the community. Letting go does not mean abandoning the community to its own fate. Quite the opposite—good sponsors and managers are actively involved in ensuring a healthy collaboration cycle. This means that they are aware of the community culture and the behaviors of community members and can from behind the scenes tune the content, capabilities, and policy enforcement of the collaboration environment to encourage desired behaviors.

In some cases, sponsors and managers may directly participate as members. But they must participate, not dominate. In fact, we have observed that through the way they behave in a community, they can provide a model for all members. The rest of the community is watching, and if your behavior demonstrates that you value them and the purpose, they will be more likely to participate. As a sponsor or manager, participate like any other community member—by offering comments, linking, and voting—to encourage and focus discussion. Expand participation by inviting interested outside parties who have a stake in the purpose of the community to join the discussion. Encourage silent participants to volunteer their thoughts. Monitor the discussion to know when to encourage the community to move forward—say, from divergent debate to convergent decision making and goal setting.

But be aware of the obvious dangers. Contributions will be colored by whatever formal authority you possess. Suggestions will be taken by some—perhaps many—as orders, preferences as directives, hints as commands, and opinions as the final word. Without meaning to, you can stifle discussion and the generation of ideas by merely expressing your personal opinion. If you feel compelled to insert your own feelings, take pains to identify them and distinguish them from whatever official opinions you might hold. The questions of if and how to participate directly in any particular community are some of the most important questions sponsors and managers must answer.

Bring an Organizational Perspective to the Community

Communities operate in the broader context of the entire organization. Their purpose and goals represent a subset of enterprise concerns. A community can become a type of special interest group and adopt an us-versus-them attitude that myopically views the surrounding world through a lens colored by self-interest. When this happens, a community can become an advocacy group and lose its ability to behave objectively and innovate. You can help avoid this by constantly bringing a broader perspective that enhances the community's ability to achieve results within the larger context. Blogs by leaders and managers are a common means for injecting a broader perspective into a community discussion.

Mark Brewer, an executive at Seagate Technology, started his blog in 2008 as a means of sharing information about progress and performance within the broader context of the whole firm.[2] In it, he raises issues regarding IT strategy, identifies gaps in performance, and presents an enterprise view about topics of the day. His blog raises rather than resolves issues and catalyzes discussion and comment that help shape decisions and actions. He does this by:

- Asking questions about the broader implications of specific community decisions and actions for the overall enterprise, its strategy, and goals

- Adding information from outside the community to broaden its customer, company, and industry perspective

- Providing his own thoughts and insights about potential pitfalls, issues, and implications of decisions and actions

In this way, Brewer provides the broader enterprise perspective communities need without dictating or directing their actions. This keeps community goals anchored in the context of the enterprise.

Build Support for Community Actions

If discussion has run its natural course without producing change, managers should take additional steps to encourage actions and changes that support the purpose. This may mean making sure that the environment adequately supports desired actions, and it sometimes may mean making direct requests for action. It's important to recognize a lack of action and make adjustments because a community not achieving purpose is a community without value to its members or the organization. If a community does not respond, you should seek to revise its purpose. If the "repurposing" fails, you may consider halting investment in the community and passively monitoring its behavior in case a valuable purpose finally emerges. In some cases, you may even disband a community. But be careful, because this drastic action can create negative perceptions in the company or marketplace.

Encourage the Emergent Nature of Communities

Emergence is one of the six principles of community collaboration and one of the most fundamental features of a community. Emergence grows out of the interactions of the collective. As members participate voluntarily, interact, achieve lower-level goals, and make decisions, exactly how they will achieve their purpose will *emerge*. As sponsor or manager, recognize that some management practices and behaviors will encourage emergence and others will stifle it.

Focus on Results, Not the Means of Achieving Results

Mass collaboration is different from other ways of working. By its fundamental nature, no one can predict or prescribe the *means* a community will choose to accomplish its purpose. Thus, no one can manage around the means of accomplishing a purpose—for example, around a detailed plan of action or a set of rules and procedures—because the means will emerge. Only outcomes can be managed.

Managers give up control to obtain the creativity of a community and ultimately its pursuit of results. Most managers would claim they are more concerned with progress—results, outcomes—than compliance with a predetermined process or plan. However, in the face of uncertainty, many managers cannot resist trying to direct day-to-day activity as well. That may work in traditional management—though it's problematic there too—but it will have a deadly effect on collaboration.

The members of a community need the freedom to choose how they will achieve the desired outcome, and they need the freedom to adapt and revise the means as they proceed and learn. An effective community that believes in its purpose will feel the need to produce results but will operate on its own timeline, determine its own interim deliverables, and figure out how its members work together. These will appear through some level of emergence. Some communities operate with implicit emergence but others more explicitly set their own goals. We have seen explicit goal setting happen in several workforce related communities, including CEMEX's alternative fuels community and at Electronic Arts. In those organizations, communities created working groups called *councils* to focus on specific actions and decisions. Sponsors and managers use these self-defined plans as a way to assess community performance.

In another example, Xilinx created a person-to-person architecture that allowed engineers to incorporate their own tools and develop their own applications for collaborating with peers and customers. In the process, the company retired its prior customer relationship management system. Giving engineers control over their own tools led to a 25 percent increase in productivity. That outcome would not have been possible if management had insisted on controlling how the engineers chose to do their work.[3]

Keep Internal Communities Safe for Collaboration

Conflict within a community is inevitable—and necessary—as ideas vie for acceptance and everyone's views are seen by everyone else, including some who will disagree strongly and say so. In most cases, community members will regulate their own and each other's behavior. After all, members are ultimately responsible for the culture of their own community. But such negative features as partisanship, blind advocacy, exclusivity, negativism, ad hominem attacks, and cliques are part of human nature and will exist even in the best-intentioned communities.

Management has a role here, for collaboration works best when members feel safe to share any and all constructive thoughts. Without that sense of security, no full and free exchange of ideas will occur, and competing ideas cannot be fully explored. Consequently, you must take action when community self-monitoring breaks down, when attacks and criticism turn personal. The goal is not to avoid conflict, which is essential to finding the best course forward, but to avoid the kind of conflict that is personal, destructive, and dysfunctional—in short, the kind that tends to stifle rather than advance collaboration.

To this end, your job as manager is to guide community interactions away from destructive conflict and toward productive and purposeful behaviors. The community sets the tone of the conversation, but management may need to keep that tone one of respect by:

- Stepping in when necessary to remind community members of organizational guidelines for community conduct

- Pressing for data and facts to support disruptive positions or contentious issues

- Encouraging inquiry ("Why do you think that?") and discouraging adamant advocacy in which members merely repeat their beliefs over and over, louder each time

- Protecting the voices of the minority, which can be drowned out by the groupthink of the majority

- Maintaining transparency—who is saying what to whom—within the community and shedding light on disruptive behaviors and side conversations

Making the community a safe place for open collaboration is everyone's responsibility. Sometimes, during the heat of discussion and debate, managers may need to remind community members of appropriate ways of interacting and reorient the conversation when it goes astray. There is a fine line between guidance and direction. One sign of a need for guidance is that community debate and discussion has slowed or even stopped because members are waiting for someone to set the tone right again or weigh in on an issue. But, once you've stepped in and discussion is back on the right track, be sure to step out—let go—again.

Keep External Communities Productively Engaged

Outside-facing communities that engage customers, prospects, suppliers, and other stakeholders place additional requirements on sponsors to keep the community productively engaged and the conversation going. Sponsors and managers have less direct influence in external communities and therefore need to influence more by facilitating and not just guiding the conversation. This most often involves ensuring the community can self-govern by making sure members understand the purpose, know policy guidelines, can rate contributions, and can flag bad behavior or inappropriate content. With these self-governing abilities in place, management then can successfully moderate the community and make adjustments to purpose messaging, policy guidelines, and policy enforcement.

In some cases, you may guide participation by direct involvement. For example, you might participate in external communities and use their own content contributions to highlight interesting ideas, create new content combinations by linking, or draw groups into the conversation. This role is seen often on Twitter, for example, where leaders retweet posts to a broader community. It also happens around individual blogs when leaders connect different views on the subject. Such interlinking can be a significant factor in building the reputation of participants and the manager, all without the manager's telling people what to do. By highlighting good participation, you can promote desired behaviors and discourage bad ones.

In addition, you can influence external communities through the way they exercise their responsibilities for the operational elements of the community, including investments made in the social media platform and the creation of authority structures as needed. Invest in productive behaviors and starve the bad.

Keep the Community Connected to the Organization

Management has a crucial role to play in helping the community function effectively within the broader context of the enterprise. The community needs organizational resources; help removing organizational obstacles, someone with the ear of leadership to speak for the community, and a way to plug community decisions into the company's formal management structures and processes.

At CEMEX, for example, the CEO conducts a formal review of each collaborative community every quarter, and community leaders represent each community and its views in executive discussions.[4] Electronic Arts has built a flexible management framework around its extensive network of communities. This structure allows communities to form organically but ensures that each has the support it needs. In fact, EA's framework is a good example of what's needed.[5]

At the enterprise level, EA has a *community champion* who facilitates the firm's overall collaborative efforts and evangelizes the benefits and goals of a communal structure within the enterprise. They also formed a *community steering committee* to oversee investments in and achievements of communities across the company. Steering committee members are from the upper levels of management and its mandate is to make sure—through better tools and resources, for example—that communities can operate as effectively as possible.

In addition, EA also creates the following positions within each community:

- A community sponsor represents each community in EA's leadership ranks. Sponsors are members of the leadership team and give the community access to the rest of EA's leadership team in order to ratify or to solicit executive support for a decision made within that community.

- A community team lead is initially nominated by the EA community steering committee, and once the community is thriving, the next team lead will eventually be elected by the community members themselves. Often a manager in the organization, the team lead facilitates the discussions and drives the efforts of the community to achieve the goals set forth by the community's charter.

If the community membership is very large, each community has the option of forming a community council. This council can form within a community to achieve specific results. Councils provide focused resources concentrating on achieving a specific goal or deliverable within a set time period. The use of councils reflects the fact that communities can grow large enough to lose their effectiveness.

EA's approach is only one of many possible, but it does illustrate the kind of structure needed to support the ongoing work of effective communities.

Create Transparency by Providing Information and Maintaining Visibility Across the Community

Transparency is a fundamental principle of collaborative communities, where everyone knows your name and sees your contributions. Avoid anonymity unless the community's purpose requires it. Transparency raises the quality of contributions as social media tools enable everyone to see, use, reuse, augment, validate, critique, and rate each other's posts. It is integral to improving content, unifying information, self-governance, self-correction, and evolution.

Transparency is also necessary for building trust in the collaborative process. Sponsors and managers support transparency in two ways: by ensuring each community has the best information to work with and by maintaining the transparency of community contributions, discussions, and decisions.

Communities need good information about their activity, progress, and results. They also need to make sure the world knows what they're doing and have accomplished. It's your job to ensure a good flow of such information within and outside of the community. This starts with seeding activities that are part of launch. Then you ensure the quality of information by paying particular attention to its sources and their validity and by identifying situations where better or more consistent information is needed to foster collaboration. Finally, you foster transparency by encouraging participation within the social media environment rather than in sidebar conversations. That can involve transcribing such content into the tool set to give everyone a chance to see and participate.

What Guiding a Community Requires of a Manager

We hope we've made two points clear: (1) collaborative communities need careful management; (2) communities will not participate and collaboration will never occur—if managers use practices that depend heavily on authority, direction, and control. For many managers, then, the launch of a community for which they're responsible will call for a personal shift in how they manage. Ask yourself questions like these to assess your own readiness to provide the kind of guidance needed:

- Are you comfortable with ambiguity about the means to achieve outcomes? Are you willing to let structure and results emerge?

- Are you able to focus on milestones and results rather than demanding detailed action plans and compliance with predetermined processes?

- Are you willing to let plans change and evolve, either when the situation changes or when community members simply discover a better way?

- Are you socially aware, and do you have the emotional intelligence needed to sense the mood and health of groups, as well as individuals?

- Are you willing to challenge accepted rules, and can you see value in alternate approaches?

- Do you have influence in your organization beyond the area where you possess formal authority? Are you influential across organizational and process lines and able to remove barriers to collaboration?

- Are you considered by colleagues to be competent in your work and field? When you speak, do others—not just those who work for you—pay attention?

- Are you a good listener? Do you let people talk? Are you truly willing to change your mind as you listen? Do you seek to understand before making a decision or even a simple judgment? Or would you rather advocate than inquire?

- Do people know your values and intentions—who you are— enough to trust you?

- Are you someone people respect and want to work with?

These are critical questions because they get at the characteristics of people who can exercise influence without relying on authority. That's key to managing a community.

Use the Principles of a Social Organization as a Guide

Communities need management just like any other coordinated effort. However, the nature of management is different in a community context. Rather than staying away or getting in the way, managers need to be involved—in the right way. As we have seen, that right way includes shifting ownership to the community, allowing the community to emerge, guiding the community rather than trying to direct and control it, and focusing on the key factors that will keep the community vital and productive.

One way to summarize this is by listing the six principles of mass collaboration—they are also the core principles of a social organization that we discussed in chapter 2—and noting for each the kind of management guidance it requires (see table 8-1).

TABLE 8-1

The principles of mass collaboration—and social organizations— and the management guidance each requires

Principle	Guiding action within the community
Participation	Encourage participation and contributions from across the community. Make the community safe for collaboration by discouraging destructive and dysfunctional behaviors and promoting productive ones.
Collective	Ensure a healthy community collaboration cycle to get the best collective results. Provide a broader perspective and help the group reach consensus and take action together as a group.
Transparency	Seed and reseed the community with the most accurate and appropriate information. Ensure that community debate, dialogue, and decisions remain visible and open to group feedback within the social environment—discourage sidebar conversations.
Independence	Watch out for groupthink and staunch advocacy by encouraging and facilitating multiple viewpoints and broader perspectives.
Persistence	Keep collaborative content, contributions, feedback, and decisions within the social media platform and easily available to community members.
Emergence	Concentrate on community results rather than trying to control the means of producing those results. Encourage the community to set its own goals and objectives, but recognize that defining the terms of engagement is a not-so-subtle form of control that will compromise community contributions.

Managers achieve superior, innovative results with collaborative communities largely by relying on forms of influence other than authority. Leadership through tools of influence other than coercion and control is a hallmark of any effective leader—and it's critical in working with a collaborative community.

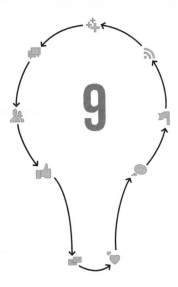

Guiding the Community's Purpose

As a global company serving local markets, CEMEX tailored its marketing and operations to local needs, in the belief that each market was unique. Company wisdom said that an effective marketing program, for example, from a developing economy would not be effective in a mature market such as Europe.

However, as CEMEX grew from 2000 to 2010, largely through acquisition, company leadership realized that some sharing of marketing approaches—value propositions—among similar markets might be useful. The company also realized that trying to foster and enable such sharing through corporate headquarters would most likely be slow, expensive, and only moderately effective.

The approach CEMEX took instead was to create, as part of its SHIFT transformation, an initiative called value proposition aligned to market needs. The initiative started in 2010 as an idea market where local CEMEX marketers could submit and share marketing approaches. For example, in rural Mexico, the company helps communities pool resources and offers microcredit to support local development. The purpose of the value proposition aligned to market needs community was to make ideas like that, along with the experience gained in using them, available to company units in other developing economies.

Within two months after the start of the idea market, 180 value propositions were in various stages of being exchanged across the organization, eventually leading to forty actual implementations. For example, CEMEX's Ready Mix operation in China submitted one value proposition but took sixty-three from other parts of the company. Mexico provided twenty-four and acquired twenty-two new ones.

The value proposition initiative succeeded far faster than anyone expected, prompting the question: With its initial purpose fulfilled, the community evolved from making everyone aware of the different value propositions to providing peer-to-peer support for taking these propositions to market. The community expanded its purpose roadmap and added webinars, blogs, and interactive dialogues in support of bringing new value propositions to new markets.[1]

This was a situation in which a community fulfilled its initial purpose—exchanging value propositions—and then went on to another related purpose that has since created radical innovations in how the company goes to market around the world. Influencing efforts toward new opportunities through such evolution of a community's purpose roadmap is what we mean by guiding the community.

Guide the Community According to Its Progress and Direction

You as sponsor or manager use purpose as a rudder for guiding the community. This involves not only keeping the community focused on its original purpose but often working with the community to fine-tune and evolve its purpose roadmap based on progress and achievements.

Guiding around purpose involves guiding the community as a whole, which is different from guiding within the community as a participant, as we discussed in chapter 8. Guiding the community via its purpose requires managers to view the community as a group, track the progress the group is making toward its purpose, assess constantly the continued value of that purpose to the organization, and look for new emerging purposes with high potential.

In this chapter, we will focus on this important task, beginning with the question: *What do you do when purpose and community no longer work together?*

When this happens, you need to reevaluate the relationship between purpose, community, and mass collaboration by asking such fundamental questions as:

- What is the relationship between the community and its original purpose? Look at how the community has interpreted its purpose and the nature of community interactions around that purpose.

- What progress has the community made against its purpose? Identify what is tangibly different for the organization now that the community is present and what new issues that progress has created.

- Has anything changed that would require reevaluating either the purpose or the community? Are there changes in the organization that require rethinking either collaborative investments or the value of collaborative outcomes? Are you building the collaborative capabilities the organization requires for continued success?

Evaluate the community's performance in two ways. First, assess its progress against the original purpose roadmap, paying particular attention to emerging directions, where the community actually focuses its energy, and the issues it discusses—all of which may signal that it's seeking to redefine itself. Second, ask these questions of yourself as the sponsor or manager at least twice a year or whenever significant change occurs in the community or its organizational context. The answers will provide valuable insight regarding the vitality and interest of community members.

Recognize When a Community Needs Adjustment

A community and its purpose can drift apart because new purposes emerge or because the community evolves and reinterprets its purpose. When those situations occur, adapt the relationship between purpose and community either by refining the purpose or by making adjustments in the community. Likewise, when the community cannot make substantial progress toward its purpose, take one or more of the following actions:

- Adjust the community according to its vitality (appeal to members) and productivity (value to the organization).

- Facilitate social circles to match participants and purpose.

- Create social circles within the community.

- Support a spin-off community to achieve a new purpose.

Guiding an active community is a never-ending process. As a sponsor or manager, you cannot, and should not try to, tell the community what it should do. Your guidance can come only from assessing progress and taking steps to bring purpose and community into better alignment.

Adjust Purpose According to the Vitality and Productivity of the Community

Both how compelling a community is to members and how useful it is to the organization can change in accordance with the business context and members' response to the purpose. Use the community's purpose and the specifics outlined in its purpose roadmap to assess both vitality and productivity—the health of the community, so to speak—and diagnose issues that may need to be addressed.

A truly productive community has three characteristics. First, its members are actively collaborating around issues related to its purpose. Second, the community is creating organizational results consistent with its purpose. Finally, it is evolving—growing in participation, defining and achieving new objectives, and engaging the rest of the enterprise.

Assess a community's health by asking questions like:

- Are members talking about issues related to its current purpose, or is it drifting?

- Is it drifting to a related or different but still worthwhile purpose? Should the organization support and encourage the new purpose—for example, by adding it to the roadmap and giving it resources?

- In community discussions, what is the ratio of new ideas to active projects? Is the community able to move from discussion to action? Do its actions reflect goals outlined on the purpose roadmap? If not, are there obstacles the sponsor can remove? Or should the sponsor revisit the purpose roadmap?

- What is the tone of participation? Is it respectful? Is there broad participation, or do a few members dominate the community? If so, is that helpful to achieving the community's purpose?

- How has the community's membership changed since the last assessment? Who has joined, and have they become active? Who has become inactive? Are the culture and purpose changing due to new entrants?

- Is the community gaining more insight into its current purpose and achieving or expanding its goals? Is it using that insight to evolve in positive directions? Does the purpose need to evolve or is it steadily delivering value to both the community and the organization?

Don't be too quick to take the community's temperature or judge it against some supposed ideal. Communities take time to coalesce.

Allow and encourage self-diagnosis where possible. One community sponsor was skeptical that a community would be effective. Rather than tell it what to do, though, he waited and watched. It took three weeks for the community to find its footing, but once it did, he was impressed with its ability to address complex issues.

The most effective community is one that is able to recognize reality and realign itself. Provide the information and contributions the community needs to assess itself and encourage improvement. Avoid attempts to impose corrective action from the outside, because this will only damage the community's ability and willingness to collaborate effectively. Encourage the community to refine its plans and commitments and to update its purpose roadmap based on its experience and actual progress.

Facilitate Social Circles to Match Participants and Purpose

Communities can involve hundreds, thousands—even millions—of people, but not every purpose will, or needs to, attract them all. A large community can achieve multiple purposes through smaller *social circles*—subgroups that form on their own around a shared characteristic, mutual concern, or common goal.

Social circles let community members specialize on smaller efforts that may not be appealing to many in the larger community. Communities at Electronic Arts form community councils, a type of inner social circle, to pursue subgoals with shorter deadlines or when the community becomes too large and loses its effectiveness. The alternative fuels community in CEMEX broke into multiple social circles to assess plant operations around the globe and identify the best performers.

Another organization, Univita, uses social circles to lend a personal approach to the challenge of caring for aging parents. This health-care services company provides common information and tools to help people assess, plan, and coordinate the needed care. It recognized that elder care is complex, personal, and not readily addressed in a single mass community. Its approach is based on building a social circle—Univita calls it a *care circle*—around a loved one. Each care circle provides a private and secure way for family members and others to share their concerns and coordinate care for a family member living alone. It supports family members with professional information and tools normally associated with mass collaboration.[2] As part of its purpose roadmap, Univita plans to expand the community so that caregivers can collaborate across care circles to share experiences and successful practices, but those purposes will come into play only after individual care circles are formed.

In a collaborative community, everyone does not do everything, but everyone can see and comment on everybody else's ideas and work. Creating social circles within the community provides a way to create greater intimacy, pursue specific aspects of a purpose, or work concurrently on different aspects of the purpose while maintaining the same overall community identity.

Without this ability, a community can splinter into subgroups that don't identify with the larger community or other subgroups. This can cause purpose divergence, conflicts, loss of motivation, and unwanted member attrition. Sponsors and managers can discourage splinter groups by:

- Identifying the work that requires a small-team approach, such as conducting a detailed investigation or developing specific recommendations and managing them alongside the community

- Enabling or encouraging social circles to form around certain issues that are not of interest to the whole community

- Applying social circles where appropriate to gain focus while continuing to share each circle's work with the entire community transparently

Forming social circles as needed within the community's social media platform can keep the community together. However, there are times when it's better to spin off part of the community to form a new community aimed at pursuing a new purpose roadmap.

Support a Spin-off Community to Achieve
a New Purpose

Communities evolve in response to new interests, changing context, and growing capabilities. In some cases, communities spawn new versions—spin-offs—of themselves. These form when some community members define a new and different purpose, attract others to join them, and their new community gets Go approval. Spin-offs are a way to accelerate the use of community collaboration because they benefit from some of the rules, tools, and members they inherit from the parent community.

While spin-offs are possible, and sometimes useful, you—as sponsors and managers—must think carefully in every case about their value. Avoid supporting a spin-off as a response to discord within a community. Rather than creating a competing community, guide members to resolve issues among themselves, even if that creates tension. Remember that the best ideas often come from constructive conflict—conflict that focuses on the merits of different approaches or ideas and never becomes personal.

Spin-offs work best when some community members create a separate grassroots effort based on a new purpose that does not fit well within the purpose roadmap of the existing community. Such a new purpose often requires new members, new content, and new functionality, and so it would not succeed as well in the original community. Spin-offs can work well for all concerned when they arise from one community success to spawn other possible successes. Look for these spin-off opportunities and use the No, Go, Grow model to determine their potential.

CEMEX faced this situation when a group of company electricians created a grassroots community on their own. They used the company's collaborative platform without a sponsor or a clearly defined purpose. Using a model similar to No, Go, Grow, sponsors decided to support this new community. As Miguel Lozano, innovation director at CEMEX, said, "I am interested in only one thing—what is good for the company."[3] Today CEMEX has more than 450 of these grassroots communities, with more than 8,000 employee participants. Some, such as the grassroots community on health and safety, has grown into a more formal structure with organization-wide impact.

Spin-offs can be useful as long as they don't produce multiple communities with essentially the same purposes that compete for resources and members. Putting ideas for spin-offs through the No, Go, Grow process can help avoid this kind of overlap and confusion. Also, avoid spin-offs that pursue the same purpose as the original community and are different only because they focus on a particular business unit, geographic region, or some other distinguishing factor besides purpose. Repeating the same purpose in a different part of the organization can easily create community silos and artificial distinctions that diminish the power of mass collaboration.

Creating a successful spin-off demonstrates the organization's ability to tap into its emerging insights and talents and rapidly scale to achieve new purposes. But allowing communities to proliferate willy-nilly will only produce confusion.

Recognize When to Reset Purpose or the Community Itself

There are times when sponsors and managers must recognize the need to, in effect, start over—for instance, when a community never forms; when one does form but cannot make progress toward its purpose and all efforts to nudge it forward fail; or when a community completes its purpose and has not surfaced and mobilized around another productive purpose. These are signs that a community needs to find a new purpose or the purpose requires a new community. Resetting a community is an opportunity for the organization to learn and improve the way it executes community collaboration.

Changing a community's purpose can alter its collaborative capacity and its ability to create results. Sponsors should recognize that adopting a new purpose changes the community and should restart the full community cycle (purpose-launch-guide) rather than simply declaring a new purpose.

Sponsors and managers face the need to reset a community when:

- Assuming a new purpose that departs from or doesn't fit well within the purpose roadmap

- Redirecting a community away from an unproductive purpose without killing collaboration

- Recovering from a significant setback

Validate significant changes in purpose or in the nature of a community using the No, Go, Grow framework. This approach helps create consistent decisions to discontinue a purpose (No), spin off a purpose into another community (Go), or refocus the community on a new purpose (Grow). Implementing any of these decisions is complex because you're now dealing not with a prospective community but a live one populated by real people.

Assuming a New Purpose

The differences between the communities Obama for America and Organizing for America illustrate the challenges of changing purpose while trying to retain the same members. Obama for America was Barack Obama's groundbreaking social media program in the 2008 election. It encompassed a unique set of collaborative communities all organized around a single purpose—securing Obama's election.

After the election, Obama for America became Organizing for America, with a new purpose: "Empowering communities across the country to bring about our agenda of change." In late 2009, Organizing for America changed again—from advocating policy to focusing on electing Democrats in the 2010 congressional elections. The community responded, participating in more than 200,000 volunteer shifts and almost 3,000 get-out-the-vote sessions around the country.[4] Yet, while these results were impressive, they were nowhere near participation levels in 2008.

Organizing a national election and pursuing a legislative agenda may seem similar because they involve many of the same people. But they're very different purposes that require different community collaboration objectives and capabilities. In fact, this is a case of when a community needs a new purpose because it's achieved its original purpose. If Organizing for America had moved from 2008 election campaigning directly to 2010 election campaigning, it most likely would have had more success because those efforts would have been much more closely aligned.

In theory, a community should disband when it achieves its purpose or its current purpose cannot attract a critical mass of participants. But the social reality is that, in a successful community, participants want to continue collaborating and so they seek a new focal point that will let them keep going—they will thus evolve its purpose. This is a good thing, and a key difference between collaborative communities and corporate initiatives. You, as a sponsoring organization, should want to maintain this asset and find a way to facilitate its continued productivity.

As we defined it in chapter 2, the purpose roadmap is a set of related purposes that define how the community's collaboration can evolve over time. It serves as a guide for developing the community by demonstrating that community collaboration can extend beyond initial objectives and goals. Consider adopting a new purpose based on the roadmap but be open to the possibility that the community may want to keep working together but needs a new direction and set of purposes.

Since social media–based collaboration is still relatively new, there are few situations where a community has met its goal and had to reinvent itself. Though it's not a social media example, the March of Dimes can provide some insight into what's required to redefine a purpose.

At its founding in 1938 by President Franklin Roosevelt, the March of Dimes was dedicated to the eradication of polio in the United States. That was its purpose, and people collaborated by donating money to fund research and treatment. (Its name came from its unique practice of painting a stripe down the middle of city sidewalks where people would lay coin donations. A dime then was the equivalent of well over a dollar today.)

By the mid-1950s, research in which the March of Dimes had played a key role produced a vaccine. As it celebrated this success, the March of Dimes also faced an existential crisis. After 1955, contributions declined because the community of donors saw that the charity's job was largely completed. By 1958, the March of Dimes had redefined its purpose to be the elimination of birth defects.

Depending on how much it differs from the current roadmap, introducing a new purpose for an existing community may require a return to the purpose and launch phases of the community collaboration cycle. Only this time, rather than working in isolation, managers and sponsors have the creative talents of an experienced community working with them.

Work with the community to define the new purpose roadmap from either the set of opportunities in the community collaboration strategy or through brainstorming sessions. Vet new purposes to ensure they represent worthwhile investments of participants' time and organizational resources. Assuming you reach a Go or Grow decision, relaunch the community by updating tool sets, seeding the environment with new content, and attracting community participants.

For the March of Dimes, success created crisis because the organization had defined a very specific purpose and never considered the possibility that it might need to find another. To relaunch itself, the charity had to establish its new purpose within the community of former donors, as well as within society at large. It first went to great lengths to thank supporters and attribute success to their donations. It then asked them to sign up for the new purpose—eliminating birth defects—by making the case that it was a natural extension of the original purpose and that continued participation would lead to similar success.

Leading an existing community beyond its original purpose involves many of the same activities. Just as the March of Dimes reinvented itself around a new purpose and retained many of the characteristics that made it successful, the community needs to relaunch itself with a new purpose and from a position of strength.

Redirecting a Community Away from an Unproductive Purpose Without Killing Collaboration

A new or different purpose suggested by the community may not be a good or appropriate one for the organization. It may represent a poor investment of the organization's resources or the community's time, talent, and attention. Discourage purposes inconsistent with the organization, its culture, or direction by emphasizing other priorities, purposes, or goals. If necessary, limit social media support. Visible antagonism or formal organizational opposition can work, but it can also rally support for the wrong purpose for the wrong reasons. In these cases, you and other sponsors and managers need to direct the community to another purpose without dictating a direction. This will be a challenge because you must find a way to redirect the community to a more appropriate purpose without damaging its collective spirit. (Reserve an outright prohibition for situations in which the emerging purpose represents an unacceptable threat to security, privacy, regulation, or the like.)

A purpose by itself is neither good nor bad; however, not all are equal in light of business strategy or vision. Use that vision and strategy as a way to eliminate purposes that possess one or more of the following characteristics:

- Purposes that do not serve the organization's customers, values, strategies, or culture

- Purposes whose success requires diminishing or compromising another division within the organization

- Purposes that are exclusive to a single group or operating unit and will create community silos

- Purposes that would require significant investment for little or no tangible business benefit

Sponsors and managers represent the organization within the community. It's your responsibility to identify when a proposed purpose is misguided, ill-advised, or dysfunctional for the organization. In the spirit of collaboration, engage the community to examine how a proposed purpose creates value for participants and the organization. That dialogue of contribution and feedback— the collaboration cycle—will give you the ability to listen and respond within the community to create a more appropriate purpose.

Ultimately, a purpose inconsistent with organizational goals or culture requires intervention. Normally that would involve having the community select another purpose. But, in extreme situations, it can lead to dissolution of the community and limiting access to collaborative environments.

Recovering from a Significant Setback

When working with collaborative communities, some failure is inevitable and natural, given the often difficult and problematic issues they are given to resolve. Reasons for failure are many—the organization or community pursued an unreasonable purpose, it failed to gain critical mass, it lacked strong or appropriate sponsorship, or the investment in social media tools for it was inadequate.

As we've said again and again, simply deploying social media technologies will rarely create community-based collaboration. Setbacks indicate the need for a deeper understanding of the target community, social media capabilities, and purpose. When setbacks occur, sponsors and managers should return to the original organizational vision for mass collaboration and refine collaborative opportunities before redefining a community's purpose and relaunching it. You have only limited time and attention to get it right.

Effective Collaboration Requires Guiding the Community

Collaboration requires structure not only within the community but also between communities and the rest of the organization. Guiding that structure is the responsibility of sponsors and managers within a social organization. Managers need to balance their advocacy for community discussions against progress the community makes toward its intended purpose and the results it achieves.

Finding the right balance between progress and purpose requires that managers lead in the collaboration effort and recognize when a community needs to change. The goal is to make such changes in ways that enhance rather than eliminate participant energy and contribution.

Given the diversity of communities, organizational culture, and community purpose, there are few hard-and-fast rules that determine when intervention is needed. Such signs as inadequate participation, dilution of effort, or a lack of progress against purpose represent opportunities to learn and adjust the community using the approaches we've described in this chapter.

Guiding the community as a unit, according to its purpose, reflects management's responsibility to create the right structures for translating individual ideas and insight into collaborative action and business-relevant results. The third and final management responsibility consists of connecting those actions with existing organizational processes and systems in order to spread the benefits of community innovation across the organization.

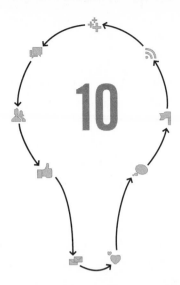

Adapting the Organization

Loyola University, in Chicago, was founded in 1870 and is the largest Jesuit university in the United States. In 2008, it created Next Stop: Loyola, a collaborative community with members comprising, above all, newly admitted freshmen, as well as members of the current freshman class and the university. The school's purpose was to help admitted students decide to enroll at the university. Next Stop was a place where they could share information about themselves, connect with other admitted students, participate in discussions, and complete the enrollment process. "Our approach is to engage the students in helping them explore Chicago as a city, Loyola as a university, and the other students who will be in their class," said Justin Daffron, SJ, associate provost for academic services.

The initiative has been a success since its introduction. Students have benefited from help in making their decision to enroll and from the chance to join a community of classmates even before arriving on campus. The university has benefited from better informed and more engaged and energized students. It has also benefited by an improvement in the percentage of admitted students who actually matriculate.[1] According to Paul Roberts, associate provost for enrollment management, "The admitted students portal, in combination with modifications to the application process, have increased our yield rate by 5 percent and decreased our melt rate by 15 percent."

On the surface, Next Stop: Loyola may look like a simple, straightforward social media application. But success required that it touch and change key parts of the entire school, including admissions, registration, student aid, housing, IT, and finance. In addition, the entire process of communicating with admitted students had to evolve. For example, school staff had to participate in community discussion forums in order to answer questions and correct student misperceptions. In addition, after some experience with the community, Loyola moved student discussion boards off the university site and onto Facebook. "We adopted the principle that we needed to be where the students are, not make the students go where we wanted them to go." said Roberts.

None of those changes just happened. They came as the result of careful and thoughtful effort by those university staff members given responsibility for the success of Next Stop. These managers had to work actively with all university departments, systems, and processes to plan the community and then make sure it worked and kept working as intended. In short, these managers had to guide virtually the entire organization toward this goal, and, while they operated with a mandate from senior leadership, they had little or no formal authority over those whose cooperation was essential.

Sponsors and managers bring to their work with a community both an organizational perspective and their own experience. They guide the community by using its purpose as both yardstick and rudder. They also guide the organization so as to productively spread community-generated ideas and innovations across the whole enterprise.

Make the Organization Safe
for Community Collaboration

Guiding the organization involves a process of facilitation, connection, and orientation that continuously links the community to organizational processes and power structures. As a sponsor or manager, you *are* these critical links. In this pivotal role, your goal is not only to satisfy the needs of individual communities but also to make the organization safe for community collaboration in general. You do this by working with organizational leaders and various, corporate functions—such as HR, IT, and finance—to build their understanding of how mass collaboration can help the organization achieve its goals. Without this understanding, these groups are likely to resist mass collaboration because they may see it as a threat to their position and authority or simply as unnecessary change.

Aligning these groups in support of collaboration is what we mean by making the organization *safe* for collaborative communities. A social organization is a safe place for mass collaboration because all elements of it recognize its value and potential. They see mass collaboration not as a threat but a means of complementing and extending the way they lead, manage, and evolve the organization.

As a sponsor or manager, you work as a catalyst with executives to build this understanding by:

- Engaging executives and senior leaders in mass collaboration activities through interlocking leadership structures—that is, leaders share responsibility for both traditional organizational activities and for the work of collaborative communities

- Extending formal processes of organizational change and governance to incorporate community results not as an experiment or novelty but as "the way we do things"

- Working with HR professionals to incorporate collaboration into the organization's definition of desired professional behavior and proper conduct

- Working with the CFO and finance to evolve budget and finance practices based on a clear understanding of mass collaboration and its resource needs. A collaborative community is unique in that it has a defined purpose but is free to define how it will achieve that purpose. This freedom reduces the effectiveness of traditional funding models and requires a different approach for budgeting and resource allocation.

- Helping IT leaders deliver collaborative capabilities that work with enterprise IT systems, maintain organizational security and operational integrity, and meet the changing needs of collaborative communities

These tasks represent a significant portion of the work performed by managers and sponsors on behalf of the communities they support.

Guide the Organization to Reduce Potential Competition and Conflict

A social organization recognizes the importance of establishing an environment in which mass collaboration can occur again and again. Organizations that treat a collaborative community as an exception or special initiative have not created the approaches for resolving the potential organizational conflict created by mass collaboration.

A community exists within the context of the organization, but its ability to function more or less independently creates the potential for competition with traditional corporate functions. Consider a community whose purpose is to find ways to improve the workplace. The potential for conflict with HR is obvious. While such a community may include HR personnel, it is not led by HR in the same way that a task force on working conditions would be.

Such tension can lead corporate functions to dismiss communities or actively oppose them. For example, in one of the companies we studied, line managers threatened by a community downplayed its launch and reinforced their traditional role with line personnel.

As a result, the launch failed when it reached only 10 percent of its target audience.

Building support for mass collaboration within the organization takes time as you work with executives, HR, finance, IT, and others to help them understand that collaborative communities support the organization rather than compete with its formal policies, processes, systems, and procedures. These groups have legitimate concerns regarding mass collaboration that need to be addressed seriously rather than dismissed with the attitude "They don't get it."

Effective managers and sponsors work with enterprise leaders to find ways of making the organization more open to the relatively unstructured nature and energy of collaborative communities. They try to reduce the organization's need for control by building confidence in the ability of communities to produce the kind of organizational value not possible using traditional methods.

Effective managers and sponsors of communities also recognize that organizational functions are responsible for the integrity of the company's people, finances, information, and systems, and they connect those concerns with community practices and activities. Without this form of active and ongoing guidance, communities will find themselves in conflict with corporate functions.

Create Interlocking Leadership Structures

Organizational guidance starts at the top and at the beginning of the approach when leaders lay out the vision for mass collaboration. In guiding executives and senior leaders around a collaborative community, you should aim to engage their support of its purpose without making them owners of the community or its work. That seems counterintuitive, since most approaches call for executives to champion an initiative. But mass collaboration is neither an initiative nor a single community. It represents a different way of operating, and executives need to be comfortable with and support that approach more than they need to champion the work of any single community.

Involving executives and leaders in the early phases—formulating vision and strategy—will help them understand the potential and limitations of mass collaboration. But that's only a start. They need to be engaged throughout the process, particularly given that communities themselves determine how they will achieve their purpose. You want the connection between executives and communities to be strong enough to build executive confidence and support but not so strong as to reduce the community's ability to participate and innovate.

Incorporate information about community progress and issues into the management routines of senior leadership. Regular updates will keep community progress visible. But avoid frequent review meetings—monthly, for example—because community progress against its purpose can be uneven. Too-frequent reporting can create a false impression of inactivity, volatility, or unpredictability. Unlike project teams and task forces, communities don't produce on a fixed timeline. Setting or allowing expectations of steady, scheduled progress will only lead to disappointment. The CEO at CEMEX, for example, conducts a formal review of each community every quarter where community leaders represent the community's views in executive discussions.

Associating a senior leader with each collaborative community is a best practice because it creates a conduit for information to flow naturally. At Electronic Arts, each community is sponsored by a member of the senior leadership team who is responsible for building organizational support for it. Management nominates community leaders, but members in each case must validate the choice through voting. CEMEX creates two points of connection. First, each initiative within SHIFT has a technical executive—a person with deep knowledge and credibility who is responsible for the quality of debate and outcomes. The second leader is a business leader who is accountable to the CEO and represents the community initiative in formal organizational systems. These forms of interlocking leadership give communities formal access to senior management without compromising their independence and open participation.[2]

Managers and Sponsors Are Buffers Between Management
and the Community

Sponsors and managers are the conduit through which social media–based innovation can grow to embrace the entire enterprise. When they fail, or are cut out of organizational decisions concerning the community, they lose influence and standing in both worlds. At the same time, sponsors are subject to the unintended consequences of management decisions, which they are responsible for resolving.

Robert Bryant (a fictitious name for a real person) is the sponsor of a blogging network at a large technology services company. The blogging network consists of about 100 people who voluntarily share their ideas, engage the public, and demonstrate the company's use of social media. The blogging network started as a grassroots community that received a Go decision because of the interest and energy of its members. In its first year, the site attracted hundreds of posts, thousands of comments, and tens of thousands of readers. The bloggers were drawing an audience, growing a web presence, and creating positive buzz for the company.

Then one of the company's clients made an acquisition. A blogger wanted to post his position on the merger with a company-sponsored blog site. Senior leadership, however, worried about the potential business risk and possible exposure to litigation if employees were making positive or negative statements on client actions. Though the community had a policy concerning blogging on clients and their products, senior leadership decided it didn't go far enough in explaining acceptable client-related posts.

The senior management team, including Bryant, agreed to work on how to revise the policy and communicate the decision to the blog community. Unfortunately, news of the planned policy changes was leaked to the blogger community. What started as a reasonable leadership decision to protect the business was now a fast growing rumor, without the proper context, on how management was stifling blogging. Confused, the blogging community responded with well over a hundred e-mails that first questioned the decision and then moved to questioning management—for example, one said, "this sounds like senior leadership doesn't understand or appreciate or want (or all three) blogging." And of course these e-mails consumed hours of professional time.

The leak created a situation that put the community at odds with senior management: the community was unhappy with a decision that seemed to come from out of the blue; senior management was unhappy because the reasons for the decision were clear to them and, after all, the bloggers were employees and the decision was made to protect the company—and the sponsor was in the middle. Rather than taking sides, Bryant demonstrated his support for both the community and the company by stepping up and taking the lead in communicating the process, engaging with senior management to help them understand the community's point of view and help bring the issue to closure.

Over a few days of intensive work, Bryant helped senior leadership understand and respond to the bloggers' questions and concerns. He helped leaders draft policy changes worded in a manner that met senior leadership's goals while minimizing restrictions on blogging. Senior leadership led the policy change and subsequent communication, but Bryant was involved from start to finish.

Bryant also worked within the community, countering rumors and making it clear that management would make a definitive announcement soon. He also met individually with particularly vocal bloggers to help them see the need for change and the reason for the business decision.

Bryant's work paid off. Senior leadership followed his advice, took comments from the community, and made greater efforts to clarify their reasoning. Community members welcomed the ability to engage senior leaders. As the sponsor, Bryant was in the middle, facilitating the process and building a bridge between the two for the benefit of both.

This situation highlights the importance of the sponsor as a conduit between collaborative communities and the organization as a whole. Without that conduit, this situation could have created a vicious cycle: the community could easily see management's decision as arbitrary and counter to the community. Management could potentially see the community as out of control and not supporting the business. Both situations were averted through the role of the sponsor and his ability to connect the community with the organization.

Work with Finance to Support Collaborative Communities

Financial planning and budgeting are important tools for coordinating and prioritizing corporate activities. However, mass collaboration can be a poor fit with finance's traditional methods of evaluation. Sponsors may prepare a more-or-less traditional business justification for a collaborative community, but the emergent properties of the community make predicting or delivering a specific ROI difficult. Couple this with the fact that the great majority of social media initiatives are abandoned, and it's easy to understand why people in finance are less than enthusiastic about funding community collaboration.

To get past this potential hurdle, community sponsors can help finance think about communities in ways that:

- *Recognize that communities are not cost-free, but that there is also a business justification for those costs:* You as a sponsor should use the business justification as a means to demonstrate results and returns. Establish reporting based on the business benefits that are closely related to the community's purpose. If the community exists to improve customer service, then predict and track how these metrics change. A control chart based on statistical process control (SPC) techniques is a tested way of showing how improvements based on community collaboration are happening over time.

- *Avoid using size ("We plan to involve all 1,200 engineers") as a primary justification for a community:* Size is often taken as a proxy for cost; a large community must therefore mean high costs. Break the assumed link between size and cost by

setting an absolute budget with a "not to exceed" figure sufficient to support community operations. This will assure
finance that cost will remain under control.

- *For workforce-based communities, address the issue of
  employee time directly:* Time taken by people involved is
  another cost factor finance uses to assess social media–based
  collaboration. They tend to see time spent collaborating as
  time away from work or as an additional burden. Point
  out where collaborating *is* or should be a normal part of
  community members' jobs already. In fact, collaborative communities are almost always a more effective and efficient way
  of doing what must be done to carry out current plans and
  meet current budgets. Communities often don't create new
  work. Instead, they provide a new and better way of doing
  the regular work that has to be done or provide a way to
  achieve valued objectives. When Gilberto Garcia, the sponsor
  of global collaboration on CEMEX SHIFT, was asked about
  the time people spent, he simply said, "Successful people
  collaborate. It's already part of their job. The rest need to collaborate in order to learn how to do their job better."[3]

- *Acknowledge that community collaboration may create new
  work for employees:* For example, facilitating client interactions in Gartner's Peer Connect community is, in fact, an additional burden on the Gartner workforce. Customer-oriented
  communities often do require some level of facilitation
  and moderating. Be realistic with these estimates. Gain the
  trust of the finance organization by demonstrating you
  understand that some communities will require additional
  employee resources and others will not and that you know the
  difference.

Keep in mind that mass collaboration typically requires less
investment than do traditional transformation projects. When you
cannot predict a precise and predetermined value, the next best thing
is to control cost. That's the logic behind establishing not-to-exceed

budgets in support of community activities. Within those limits, sponsors and managers are responsible for guiding an investment and ensuring it's well spent.

Work with Human Resources to Support Collaborative Communities

How do you ensure that employees behave appropriately on social media? How do you distinguish when someone is acting as an employee and when that same person is acting as a private individual? How do you control the information people share and make sure it doesn't conflict with the corporate message or reflect poorly on the company? How do you protect your corporate intellectual property and brand from unauthorized use?

The Windsor Locks Board of Education in Connecticut recently forced a school superintendent to resign after he commented on Facebook that he slept in until 10 a.m. on his first day on the job. He also posted details about counseling an administrator to retire or face termination.[4]

A waitress in Charlotte, North Carolina, was fired for making disparaging remarks on Facebook about a customer who, after hours of receiving service, left a small tip.[5] Three New York City teachers were fired for flirting with students on Facebook.[6] Such events are so common that, in fact, there's a Facebook group, called Fired by Facebook, with more than three hundred members who exchange stories about how Facebook postings led to their dismissal.[7]

The social Web throws up these and other policy challenges that highlight the need for organizations to establish policy for social media behavior. We don't cover the details of formulating such policies in this book because covering the material adequately would demand a book of its own. But be aware that there are some good resources available.[8] Your legal and HR departments should approve any policy or rule, while public relations and marketing should vet policies and rules involving customers, suppliers, or other nonemployees.

HR professionals should make clear that workplace policies and standards of professional conduct extend to whenever and wherever an employee can be identified or associated with the company, which includes:

- Employees participating in a corporate-run Web site, even when that participation involves content normally considered personal or private—for example sharing childcare tips on an internal community website.

- Corporate-run sites, where the expectations for professionalism and appropriate behavior should be the same as those that apply to any corporate location, real or virtual.

- Third-party social sites, such as Facebook, LinkedIn, or YouTube, where employees can participate for both corporate and personal purposes. These sites often represent gray areas. Effective guidelines here revolve around whether individuals either identify themselves as employees or act in their professional roles. For example, when a salesperson is promoting his company's products in Facebook, he is acting as an agent of the company even if he does not explicitly identify himself as an employee.

- Whenever individuals identify themselves in ways that reasonably tie them to the company. This can include, but isn't limited to, profiles that name the company as employer, profiles that link to company sponsors or company-affiliated work groups, or pictures that show the employee wearing the company logo or that were taken at work.

The appendix presents a sample outline of guidelines that illustrate the type and level of policy guidance for social media participants.

Incorporate monitoring procedures when you create a policy. Include the three common monitoring approaches associated with social media:

- *Automated tools:* Automated tools can be set to either delete inappropriate messages or images immediately or highlight such messages for review.

- *Self-monitoring:* With social self-monitoring, members keep an eye on themselves and each other, using social media tools to highlight inappropriate behavior and assigning it to the individual involved.

- *Direct involvement:* While the community is encouraged to police its own behavior, there are situations when acceptable community standards fall below your organization's expectations of professional behavior. This is where managers become the front line in using their judgment to distinguish between acceptable and unacceptable online behavior.

Evaluate and Reward Performance in a Collaborative Environment

For workforce-oriented communities, how do you incorporate the voluntary contributions of community participants into their performance evaluation and rewards? Sponsors and managers work with HR professionals to establish appropriate policies for governing behavior within collaborative communities.

HR has an ongoing role in performance management and rewards. Performance management measures specific job outcomes, skills, behaviors, attitudes, and actions related to performance. Evaluating an individual's contribution to the community involves extending these elements of job performance to include:

- *Building relationships:* A productive member of a collaborative community builds both formal and informal professional networks; maintains and extends networks within, across, and outside organizational boundaries; obtains and shares information, ideas, and problems; and solicits advice, support, and commitment that helps the development of mutually acceptable solutions.

- *Communicating for results:* A productive collaborator expresses technical and business concepts, ideas, feelings, opinions, and conclusions well, both orally and in writing;

reinforces words through tone and empathetic body language; and listens attentively.

- *Demonstrating flexibility:* A productive collaborator responds appropriately to changes in the work environment and emerging opportunities; balances risks and reprioritizes; adapts to new, different, or changing situations, requirements, or priorities; shows an understanding and appreciation of individual differences; and works effectively with diverse persons and groups.

- *Seeking information:* A productive collaborator gathers and analyzes information on current and future trends or best practices; seeks information on issues influencing the progress of organizational and process issues; and translates up-to-date information into activities that improve performance.

While social media provides new settings for evaluating these qualities in action, these settings do not preclude the role and responsibility of community sponsors and managers. Such tools as 360-degree reviews and peer-to-peer evaluations are all possible, but they may not be efficient or effective at assessing performance. Relying exclusively on such self-evaluation can lead to a popularity contest rather than a frank discussion of the issues. HR and managers need to create an environment that encourages the freedom to express contrarian views, views that are so often suppressed in the formal work environment but are a critical strength of community collaboration.

Community sponsors and managers should take advantage of tools built into most social media technologies that measure each member's contribution to the community in terms of posts, comments, votes, and other participation metrics. This information adds a quantitative component to what would otherwise be an essentially qualitative evaluation.

An effective HR department understands the fluid nature of collaboration and the importance of behavior and action over policy, hierarchy, and standards. The result is a set of revised HR policies that recognize the fluid, undefined, and unstructured nature of work in a collaborative context.

Rewards

Collaborative communities need new forms of reward and compensation that reflect the value and importance of contribution in a collaborative community. Here are some rules of thumb:

- Avoid setting targets or quotas for social media participation because the perverse and unintended effect of such a policy is to denigrate what is supposed to be a voluntary effort.

- Emphasize nonmonetary rewards. For example, have individual members represent the community in executive meetings, feature their ideas in company publications, and formally recognize their contribution on the company's Web site.

- Provide for spot rewards in the form of bonuses to active participants when their community produces tangible results. Be careful to recognize exceptional contribution based on demonstrable criteria and performance; otherwise, the tendency to include everyone makes rewards a common expectation.

- Incorporate community contribution and collaboration into performance evaluation and promotional decisions and let people know that it is one of the selection criteria. This approach connects community activity with career development in ways that recognize and value collaborative behaviors.

Community sponsors and managers provide a connection between technical HR policies and social interactions within a community. They are the conduits for transmitting how policies and behaviors apply in the world of social media, and they use their judgment in determining when and how community behaviors support or conflict with the organization's values and standards.

Members of externally oriented communities require different motivators. Ideally, the act of participating and accomplishing a shared purpose will be enough to motivate participation and the right behaviors. However, there is participation and there is participation. You may need to use incentives to motivate greater levels of contribution. There are four mechanisms often used for this purpose. If you use none of them, don't be surprised if people don't play.

- *Make it fun:* Participation can provide enjoyment to participants. The world is moving quickly down the road of using games in a variety of settings. Get on that road yourself. If you think productivity can't (or shouldn't) be fun, then you shouldn't be building environments for community collaboration.

- *Solicit ways to improve the environment:* The act of participating can make the environment easier to use. This principle is often applied when asking for feedback. For example, if you ask people to rate content—say, by rating it on a 1–5 scale—make the ratings useful to them. Let them sort by rating. Build in a recommendation engine that suggests what other content they might like. That way members benefit personally as well when they supply a rating.

- *Provide social incentives:* A social incentive gives the recipient status in the community. Recognizing productive behaviors and valuable contributions through mechanisms like leader boards, level titles, badges, and the like are becoming more and more common in social media environments. People like to excel. It's human nature. Use it.

- *Run contests and hand out awards:* These can be traditional "limited time" contests where winners receive a prize. But they can also be nontraditional and ongoing. People love points. Uncover what matters to participants and give them whatever that is.

Work with IT to Create the Right Experience by Customizing the Community's Tools

Community collaboration challenges the IT organization because social media technologies often allow communities to build their own applications and collaborative platform. While any community can assert greater control of the technology it uses, building applications in this way occurs more often in communities of employees working on internal projects. In these situations, community members can tailor the social media environment in their own way faster and cheaper than IT.

Community customizations are driven by the community according to their need and delivered by the community according to their capability. For example, at high-tech engineering company Xilinx, engineers use a person-to-person architecture that includes resources that help them customize their tools to support the way they work. At CEMEX, individual communities customize their tools; for example, an application for capturing community specific information or the use of video to help them work more effectively. Loyola University incorporated students directly in the development process for building a community of admitted students.

Communities customize the content rather than the code, giving them a sense of self-determination and control that supports greater participation and responsibility. IT creates the technical and operational platform that supports customization and mass collaboration. Sponsors work with IT to build the initial social media environment and evolve it to changes in community needs and gain their support for the communities' needs, including the need to tailor and customize the environment on their own. An unsupportive IT function can stand in the way of collaboration by claiming that social media is unsecure, unstable, or unproductive because it's not part of standard corporate systems. Building a community-customizable environment can support more than immediate needs.

Xilinx provides an example of how an IT perspective can bring an added dimension to these tools. The company wanted to improve productivity by fostering collaborative communities of its customers and design engineers. It had a full complement of enterprise systems; however, CIO Kevin Cooney knew that Xilinx engineers created and consumed large amounts of unstructured information in the form of e-mails, diagrams, and notes—information that would need to be accessible to support collaboration.[9]

Rather than forcing collaborators to work only with corporate systems, Cooney created a person-to-person set of collaborative tools that work alongside corporate systems, including the means for engineers to customize for their own needs the content shared among themselves and with customers.

The results were impressive: significant improvement in the productivity of engineering support and increased quality of customer solutions. According to Cooney, "Engineer productivity has increased because the architecture reduces collaborative overhead. More importantly, the ability of engineers to rank solutions defines which solutions are the most effective. This raises productivity and customer value by allowing engineers to leverage the highest-rated solutions as starting points for new designs. These solutions may seem technically simple, but the applications are complex and the results are strategic."

Social organizations recognize that traditional IT processes cannot keep up with the diversity or pace of social media demand. Rather than becoming a bottleneck to collaboration, CIOs in these organizations support innovation and collaboration by:

- Providing a platform of social media tools that support community requirements for usability and ease of content creation. IT works with the community to understand its needs and to share innovations across communities.

- Evaluating technologies identified by the community and ensuring that these tools possess sufficient security as well as functional and technical compatibility with the existing environment.

- Hosting community applications by taking advantage of elastic services—cloud infrastructure or SaaS, for example—to meet the storage and bandwidth requirements of these applications.

It's easy for IT and others to see collaborative communities, mass collaboration, and social media as technologies and therefore part of their responsibility. IT needs to be involved because it participates in creating and operating the collaborative environment, but sponsors and managers must work with IT to create environments for collaboration and to foster the recognition that these environments are different from, not competitors with, core IT systems.

Security: Instill a Personal Sense of Responsibility

Security is a constant concern with collaboration and a potential sticking point for a community. The exclusive nature of security—for example, restrictions on who has access to certain information—runs counter to the inclusive nature of mass collaboration. Technology provides a partial answer to collaboration-based security problems and should be incorporated into social media requirements during launch. However, placing all responsibility for security on technology will create restrictive systems that destroy the openness needed for collaboration. "Trust but verify" is a common theme in security regimes that also applies to community collaboration. Community leaders, managers, and members should be encouraged to monitor and take responsibility for their own and each other's behavior.

The tension between security and openness need not restrict community collaboration. Rather, it requires a blended approach that leverages security technology in combination with community commitment to keeping collaboration secure *and* the conversation open.

In a blended approach, emphasize the notion of qualifying people seeking to participate in the community. Open communities such as Facebook, LinkedIn, or Amazon assume participants to be trustworthy until their actions prove otherwise. Those whose behavior is deemed abusive, untrustworthy, or unhelpful are either ignored or, in the extreme, removed from the community.

A different approach is to create communities with limited access in which new members must be invited to join and participate by existing members. Those members who invite others to join are putting their reputations on the line. New participants who misbehave or contribute little to the community will diminish not only their own status but their sponsors' as well.

Transparency plays an important role here. The collaboration platform should provide an audit trail of all community discussions and contributions. As one executive put it, "Collaboration requires open communication lines, but open lines do not require anonymity."

Review communications patterns to identify potential security risks, looking particularly for situations where members have access to sensitive information. Look too at increased downloads of data or situations where information is sent outside the company. While there may be legitimate reasons for these activities—for example, new members frequently trip monitoring alarms as they try to catch up with their peers—these tools are a useful way to identify behavior that needs investigation.

Build Links Between the Community and Organizational Processes

Once communities are launched, they will need ongoing guidance throughout their lives. A significant portion of this guidance will take the form of creating links between each community and the broader organization. These links work in both directions—to keep the community vital and productive and to feed the value created within the community to the entire organization. The ability to create strong two-way links is a basic competence of the social organization.

A social organization incorporates mass collaboration in its governance processes. Governance concerns the design and assignment of decision rights. A social organization faces multiple decisions that benefit from a structured governance approach, an approach that links decisions at the community and organizational levels through governance. These decisions include:

- *Mass collaboration and social media principles:* The definition of community-based collaboration, its scope, goal, and role in the rest of the organization. These arise through the visioning process and are best agreed to by an executive committee.

- *Collaborative strategies and objectives:* The specific directives, goals, and decisions that define your direction in the use of mass collaboration. These decisions shape the nature and boundaries of mass collaboration and should involve executives and social media sponsors as part of the strategy.

- *Purpose and organizational needs:* Decisions revolving around the assignment of purposes and approval of a community's purpose roadmap. These decisions start with community sponsors and early community participants.

- *Community formulation governance:* These are the decisions that drive the No, Go, Grow model in determining the approval and level of investment of proposed communities.

- *Mass collaboration policy and guidelines:* Decisions about the policies that govern collaborative activities that define the accepted and desirable behaviors among contributors.

- *Collaborative infrastructure and tools:* The social media technologies that form the basis for mass collaboration channels and the technology platform. These technical decisions should involve social media sponsors and CIO/IT working in a steering committee.

- *Organizational initiatives, investments, and priorities:* Decisions concerning which community solutions and initiatives should be adopted across the organization. These investment decisions are made following arrangements similar to those that apply to other organizational change initiatives.

Clear governance arrangements establish the relationships and expectations between collaborative and organizational decisions concerning the community's purpose and how it fits within the broader context of strategic planning and execution. Community sponsors and executives use these arrangements throughout the life of the community to structure decision making and actions surrounding the overall social media initiative.

Expand Community Innovation into Company Transformation

Communities collaborate to define new solutions, share practices, and explore issues. They cannot raise capital, allocate operational resources, or mandate changes in the way the company operates. Those functions are reserved for the organization's leadership and formal management structures. To effect organizational change, a community needs to connect with those structures as soon as achieving its purpose leads it to reach outside the community itself.

An effective organizational governance structure establishes the way the community operates within the context of the rest of the organization. Governance principles and strategies should define when a community's initiative extends it directly into the broader organization. Such an extension is a critical moment in the operation of the community and represents a major payoff for the organization's investment in collaboration.

Collaborative communities exist alongside the organization's formal structure. Communities such as CEMEX's alternative fuels community can exchange information, share equipment settings, and highlight proven practices. But the community alone cannot dictate organizational, plant, operational, or structural changes needed to achieve its purpose at the scope and scale of the whole organization. Moving from community generated ideas to organization action requires connecting community ideas and recommendations with formal management processes and authority. Transitioning from the community to the company takes deft leadership and management to maintain community interest, involvement, and ownership.

Community sponsors and leaders achieve this by:

- Maintaining each community's relationship with the organization's formal structures and processes. At CEMEX, quarterly reviews with the CEO provide one way.[10] Seagate Technology keeps the entire company informed by publishing its performance via a community wiki that has more external than internal subscribers.[11]

- Fostering recognition within the community that achieving the community's purpose will require making changes outside the community. Leaders do this by encouraging the community to think beyond its current membership, engaging other interested parties, and asking what's needed to fully achieve results. Electronic Arts' IT community, for example, makes decisions that require support and coordination across the organization.

- Involving the community in defining the scope of an organizational initiative, including associated business needs, business justification, and high-level design. This extends community thinking directly into the organizational initiative. The alternative fuels community within CEMEX, for example, defined a five-year strategy that encompassed the entire organization, not just the community itself.[12]

- Adopting more formal and structured change processes, tools, and techniques as the initiative moves from community-centric to organization-centric. Communities can continue to use collaborative tools as part of the change process. However, moving beyond community initiatives will require more formal organization-wide processes and structures.

- Encouraging community leaders to become leaders of the organizational initiative. This directly connects the community and organization at a personal and professional level. Rather than handing over their ideas to others, community leaders leap back into more formal structures to drive organizational change. Such a move builds credibility with enterprise leaders as they see communities working with rather than against the organization.

Sponsors extend the community into organizational change processes more than they formally hand over responsibility for the change. Extending community initiatives in this way represents an organizational return on the initial investment in social media and community collaboration. It also represents one of the ways collaborative communities demonstrate how they contribute directly to improved organizational performance.

In a social organization, your task as manager or sponsor of guiding communities and the organizational context in which they operate is never-ending. Unless conditions within communities and the broader context are right, unless strong ongoing links bind both communities and the enterprise, communities will be less likely to succeed; and, even if they succeed locally, the value they create will remain local, unavailable to the entire organization.

Effective Guidance Establishes the Basis for the Social Organization

Management is responsible for the productivity of the processes within mass collaboration and is an essential element in becoming a social organization. It contributes to mass collaboration success at every level by working in the middle of the community, by overseeing the relationship between the community and its progress against its purpose, and finally by connecting the community with the organization. All three levels contribute to building mass collaborative capabilities and executive confidence in collaborative communities to achieve valued results.

Guiding the organization is a complex and ongoing process that starts at the beginning—during visioning and strategy setting. It continues throughout the collaboration cycle as managers connect and engage organizational functions in support of community collaboration. Managers connect a community with the company, which not only energizes the community but also validates the effectiveness of mass collaboration when community improvements go viral throughout the organization and customer base.

Managers who cannot make this connection can still create significant value within the community itself. However, that value will be limited to the bounds of the community. Making the organization safe for community collaboration defines the difference between a single successful initiative and the ongoing use of mass collaboration. That difference is the essence of how management and mass collaboration come together to create the social organization.

The Path to Becoming a Social Organization

I N THE NEAR FUTURE, every company and organization will need to come to terms with the phenomenon of social media. Employees, customers, and other stakeholders will expect and demand it. This disruptive technology—and we're only beginning to discover how disruptive it will be—promises to bring changes that can now be foreseen only dimly.

We hope we've convinced you that more will be required than the now-common practice of provide-and-pray, in which organizations simply make social technologies available with the expectation that good things will happen spontaneously. They won't in almost all cases unless you start by understanding and embracing four fundamental success factors:

- *It's about the masses:* Enabling mass collaboration is what makes social media unique and transformational. Mass collaboration requires the combination of three components: social media, community, and purpose. It's more than a technology.

- *Make the purpose matter:* Mass collaboration rarely happens by itself. That's why simply providing the technology almost always fails. Technology doesn't attract participants—and without participation and contribution, there's no community. If a community does form by chance, it rarely does anything useful for the sponsoring organization. You must actively nurture mass collaboration around a compelling purpose that is both meaningful to the participants and produces value for the enterprise.

- *Adhere to the six principles:* A group that collaborates, no matter how large the group, doesn't necessarily equal mass collaboration. To be truly collaborative, a community must possess six defining characteristics or principles: *participation, collective, transparency, independence, persistence,* and *emergence.* Take away any one of them and the activity is no longer mass collaboration.

- *Repeat and embed in your organization:* Mass collaboration should not be treated as another organizational tool but made a core competence that's woven into the fabric—processes, culture, systems, and practices—of your firm. The goal is to become a social organization so that, when facing any problem or opportunity, you and your colleagues throughout the firm always ask, "Would a community be a better way to deal with this?" If the answer is yes, you're able to use mass collaboration to tap into the knowledge, experience, creativity, and passion of all those involved.

And remember—social organizations develop over time. One successful collaboration community is not enough. The vast majority of companies featured in this book didn't get it right the first time. We know from the companies we've studied ourselves that the ability to tap the creative knowledge of customers and employees again and again comes from the right social media attitude and capabilities.

The technologies that enable mass collaboration require a strong proactive approach if you hope to realize its full potential. It takes more than adding a Facebook page and Twitter account to your communications channels or installing a social media team in your marketing organization. It takes more than formulating a new set of policies to address social media behavior. What's required is much more basic: a social organization operates differently because it thinks differently and sees the world differently. Committing to this proactive approach will change your organization in fundamental ways.

Getting from Here to There

We've spent the vast majority of this book describing the capabilities of a social organization and why you should strive to become one. But how do you get there? To make progress, you need to start by recognizing where you are now.

In chapter 4, we introduced the six F system of categorizing organizational attitudes toward social media: folly, fearful, flippant, formulating, forging, and fusing. These categories actually define the path for evolving into a social organization. However, they don't represent a straight linear progression. Those organizations in any of the first three stages—folly, fearful, or flippant—should move directly to the formulating stage. From there they move from formulating to forging and, ultimately, to fusing. What's involved in these three milestones is a sequential evolution that combines gaining momentum, developing successful practices, changing culture, and altering operations that will occur only with diligent effort, time, and experience (see figure 11-1). You are a social organization when fusing begins. To get there, determine your organization's current position in this progression and then plot your path forward.

The path to becoming a social organization begins when you achieve a formulating attitude and move beyond seeing social media with fear, folly, or flippancy. Each of these attitudes reflects a limited understanding of social media and the management tools needed to realize its potential. Leading a social media initiative starts with correcting these attitudes and establishing the platform for mass collaboration.

FIGURE 11-1

A progression path to becoming a social organization

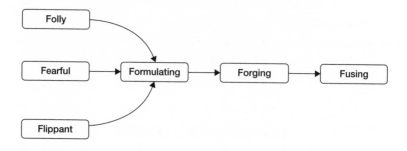

Source: Anthony J. Bradley, "The Business Impact of Social Computing on Company Governance," Gartner Inc., September 11, 2008.

Does Your Organization See Social Media as Folly?

Organizations in a folly stage primarily consider social media a source of entertainment with little or no business value. Leaders with this attitude usually ignore social media by saying it has no real business application or isn't relevant to their industry or business model. If your organization sees social media as a fad, something that has no place there, a waste of time, then you're in the folly stage.

Consider the following ways to help your organization see the potential of social media and begin moving from folly to formulating:

- Examine how much the organization is already using social media. The extent of current use will probably open some eyes and capture attention. Look for the number of employees on Facebook, Twitter, LinkedIn, and similar sites. See how many unofficial company Facebook pages, Facebook groups, LinkedIn groups, Twitter accounts, Wikipedia articles, and the like are already up and running. Chances are, you have a substantial social Web presence already, whether you know it or not. Find out how big it is. Examine how people are using these directly relevant communities and why. Assess whether current use is good or bad for the company and how you might turn it into a more valuable asset.

- Investigate competitive reasons for pursuing community collaboration. Explore what your competitors are doing and how new entrants in your industry are competing. Don't be surprised if some of them are beginning to use social media to differentiate themselves. Identify ways social media might provide competitive advantage or create a competitive necessity in your business.

- Examine opportunities to apply community collaboration to some of the more prominent business challenges in your business (see chapter 4 on vision). Because your organization doesn't recognize the business value of social media, it's critical to identify opportunities that are easily justifiable in business terms and have a relatively high chance of success. To move forward in these areas, you will need to build a compelling, clear, and measurable business justification.

- Use the information developed in the steps above to get the ear of key business leaders and convince them the organization needs a strategic approach to community collaboration.

- Don't spread yourself too thin. Focus on succeeding with one or two community collaboration efforts and create momentum around early successes.

Remember, you defeat folly by replacing it with fact. Executives cannot support what they don't understand. You're more likely to succeed if you approach them not as an advocate or true believer but as someone whose prime concern is the sustained health and success of the firm.

Is Your Organization Fearful?

Where fear of social media predominates, leaders see it as a threat to productivity, intellectual capital, security, privacy, management authority, or regulatory compliance. Organizations with this attitude know that social media has potential, but they're convinced its risks outweigh its benefits. Often, they take their lead from the legal, security, or regulatory compliance departments that, because of what they're paid to worry about, are understandably reluctant to pursue social media.

In this stage, the organization actively discourages and even explicitly prohibits the use of social media. It erects barriers to social media that range from limiting access to social media sites to an outright ban on its use. If your organization dismisses social media and severely limits or prohibits its use—and justifies these actions by pointing out all the potential risks and obstacles and citing high profile failures or instances of bad behavior—then your organization fears social media.

To replace fear with a new formulation of mass collaboration, take the following actions:

- Find opportunities to apply community collaboration to business challenges where risks are minimal and business value is clear. In fearful organizations, safety trumps business value, so choose low risk over high business value, particularly in the beginning.

- Attitudes can vary across organizations, so look for social media opportunities in areas where leaders are less fearful. Figure out who in the management and leadership ranks is resisting social media use, assess their influence on the opportunities you want to pursue, and create a plan to address their concerns throughout the effort.

- Complete a risk-versus-reward analysis for select purposes. Fearful organizations are most aware of social media risks, but most likely they're much less aware of the potential benefits. And they're certainly even less knowledgeable about the risks of *not* pursuing social media. Bring all the elements of risk and reward forward for a more balanced viewpoint and better-informed decision making. Above all, don't ignore or minimize the risks. Instead, recognize them and address them directly.

- You will need to sell your way out of the fearful stage; so, as in the folly stage, see what competitors are doing—or not doing—and examine competitive opportunities and threats.

- And as when dealing with folly, don't try to do too much. Change your culture gradually over time. Don't shoot for one big effort that will change everyone's mind. Start small and build momentum, success on success. Some organizations purposely start with workforce-facing community collaboration to mitigate the risk and ramifications of social media failure or bad behaviors.

Fact and experience are the most effective way to drive out fear. The actions outlined above start that process. Indeed, that process may have to start with you as a pioneer who demonstrates the advantages of using social media. That has been Mark Brewer's experience at Seagate Technology. He was the first executive to use blogging and wikis to publish and carry on collaborative discussions around the performance of his group. He was able to demonstrate that the use of social media did not produce social mayhem.

Is Your Organization Flippant About Social Media?

A flippant organization no longer ignores or fears social media, but it doesn't take it seriously either. Usually, a flippant company neither stands in the way nor supports social media actively. It simply makes the technology available with little direction for using it, other than perhaps some basic policy guidance, in hopes that productive communities will form spontaneously and deliver value to the organization. This stage is where the provide-and-pray practice thrives, producing widespread failure.

A flippant organization often starts with marketing, where it tries to capitalize on the social Web as another communications channel. It talks about Facebook pages, Twitter accounts, YouTube channels, and the like as a way to expand its messaging on the Web. These steps aren't by themselves bad, as long as the company realizes it's only dipping its toe into this new capability. It will never be a social organization if it limits itself to using social media for marketing communications. Its IT organization may implement new social media tools as part of the infrastructure, but without any clear, defined purpose. This focus on technology will stall, and can outright halt, progress toward becoming a social organization.

To progress beyond the flippant stage, an organization must move from social media as a technology platform to social media as a business solution. It must shift from ad hoc and reactive steps to a planned and proactive strategy. Key steps for making this move include these:

- Seek out, examine, publicly recognize, and endorse any successes that have emerged. But acknowledge and position these successes as exceptions in a sea of poor results and point out that a strategic approach can deliver more consistent success. Consider estimating the cost of the failures, but be careful not to cast all community collaboration in a poor light. Above all, don't bring up the cost of failures unless you have shining examples of success. The key point to make tactfully is that social media can deliver real business value but that the company is currently falling short of the potential because it lacks a vision and strategy.

- Find a willing business unit and actively accomplish some one-off successes. Companies flippant about social media aren't quick to jump in and support an effort, but they also don't put up big roadblocks. This is a major benefit compared with the folly or fearful stages. So although you may not be able to talk leadership into an organizational vision and strategy, you may be able to operate somewhat strategically at lower levels and begin blazing a path forward.

- As with folly and fear, you will need to sell your way out of the flippant stage. So investigate what competitors are doing and talk in terms of competition and competitive advantage. Unlike folly and fear, however, where progress will require a significant shift in mind-set, convincing leaders to move beyond flippancy should be an easier sell. Focus on the capabilities you've already developed, along with any successes to date, and position the move to the formulating stage as the next step in a natural progression.

Combating a flippant attitude involves a combination of proof and patience. The steps above will help you educate your organization about the realities of social media and its role in mass collaboration. Creating proof through a successful application is necessary but not sufficient to change a flippant attitude. Only when others see the benefits of a proactive approach to social media for themselves will your organization move to formulating the attitudes needed in a social organization.

Have You Become a Formulating Organization?

A formulating attitude is the first step in becoming a social organization. An organization in this stage recognizes the potential of social media for addressing strategic needs and generating durable change. Organization leaders demonstrate this recognition by endorsing and participating actively in the steps we've outlined in this book. They contribute to an organizational vision and strategy for social media. They fund a social media platform and recognize the need to integrate community collaboration into other activities.

Xilinx and Electronic Arts each use community collaboration to achieve strategic goals. Xilinx has created a community of customers and design engineers to work with customers, leverage engineer knowledge, and capture unstructured information to increase their productivity and improve the quality of custom designs. Electronic Arts established cross-company communities that provide the benefits of coordinated decision making while preserving the independence required for creativity and innovation.

What separates a formulating attitude from the next level, forging, is that a formulating organization hasn't yet developed the capabilities needed for consistent, repeatable success with social media across the enterprise. Business application, practices, and success with social media varies, often significantly, from one business unit and department to the next. To make progress, a formulating organization must build on the success of individual collaboration efforts to develop the organizational skills needed for more and grander efforts by taking the following actions:

- Dissect social media successes and failures and catalogue why they succeeded or failed. Turn what you learn into a set of practices to repeat and those to avoid. Use these practices as a foundation for improving companywide performance with community collaboration.

- Publicly and loudly promote community success and recognize and reward individual contributors who made extraordinary efforts and contributions. After a string of successes, revise your community collaboration vision to increase the rate at which you pursue community collaboration projects. Also, evaluate how many grassroots Go efforts are under way and encourage more if needed.

- Create a new set of baseline measures of social media success. Improve your ability to capture and communicate the real business value produced by community collaboration.

- Improve and expand organizational structures that support collaboration. Place a more senior leader in charge of those structures. Put in place a community and council for identifying and sharing best practices. Create a center for building collaboration competence throughout the organization.

- Create a formal effort that seeks ways to change the organization through wide participation in community collaboration.

- Make sure all leaders and managers in the organization are fully informed about community collaboration, including the benefits it's already providing and its future potential.

These actions move mass collaboration into executive and management processes, which will give it the capability of raising performance across the enterprise.

Are You Forging the Capacity to Use Mass Collaboration Strategically?

Organizations with a forging attitude support and encourage the use of community collaboration in people's everyday work across the organization. Forging requires broad executive support. More important, it will only take root in an organization where people feel safe to collaborate in communities. In a forging organization, people at all levels believe mass collaboration is more than possible—it's the preferred way to address organizational challenges and opportunities.

CEMEX provides a good example. Through its SHIFT initiative, the company operates multiple communities that focus on purposes derived from its corporate strategy. The executive team has embraced mass collaboration—developing and sharing innovative ideas across the worldwide firm—as the means to pursue strategy and break down organizational barriers. These approaches are characteristics of a forging organization, as well as important sources of the results CEMEX is realizing.

A forging organization is on its way to becoming a social organization. It possesses the capabilities for mass collaboration, as well as management support for deploying these capabilities across the enterprise. It has several community collaboration successes under its belt, and best practices are widely shared. Leaders have confidence in the ability of communities to pursue a meaningful purpose. They understand that social media can be applied in different ways in specific situations. They know when mass collaboration won't work and can make decisions about which communities Go and which require investment to Grow. They allow and encourage a diversity of collaborative efforts, from large communities to smaller, grassroots centers of interest. CEMEX, for example, through SHIFT supports both the communities that pursue corporate strategies and, in addition, hundreds of grass roots communities.

Repeated collaboration success in a forging organization has produced the widespread support of leaders and managers. Only one step remains before it can advance to the fusing stage, where it becomes a truly social organization. It must embed a community collaboration mentality in its corporate support organizations, such as HR, IT, legal, and finance.

To achieve that step, take these actions:

- Document the corporate obstacles encountered in pursuing community collaboration, such as processes, systems, management practices, policy, standard practice, and so on. Assess how they hinder greater success. Then change them.

- Incorporate the principles of mass collaboration into product development processes and systems—make your *products and services* more social—to attract and engage the next generation of customers.

- Evaluate the working relationships between community collaboration efforts and business functions such as finance, IT, HR, and legal. Take specific actions to improve these relationships.

- Add to your hiring criteria in all parts of the enterprise an affinity for social media and community collaboration. Do this especially for leaders and managers.

- Ensure the way you evaluate and compensate all employees accounts for participation in collaborative communities. Look in particular for a willingness to share knowledge and ideas rather than hoard them. Move the corporate culture to one where it is commonly understood that every employee's value to the company is much more than what they know. It's what they share.

- Develop ways that connect innovation and ideas arising from collaboration community with organizational change processes. This is critical if you want to leverage innovation across the organization.

Are You a Fusing Organization—a Social Organization?

A fusing organization is one in which mass collaboration is embedded in the way leaders lead and the whole organization thinks and works. We have studied many brick-and-mortar organizations that are starting to develop a fusing attitude, but we've not yet seen one that has fully fused mass collaboration into its organizational DNA.

Fusing organizations treat community collaboration as an integral part of their work. It's simply how they do things. So powerful is this attitude that in a true social organization the need for an explicit community collaboration vision and strategy subsides. All business strategy and execution already includes community collaboration wherever appropriate.

Everyone Is Getting Social, Including You

Our goal is to help you build on these basic concepts and become a social organization. That requires starting small and building success on success, developing along the way the necessary organizational skills and culture. You may have already started down this path, overcoming initial concerns and early efforts. Keep going. You may be recovering from the lackluster results of a provide-and-pray approach. Get better. You may be wondering how to go beyond initial successes. Stay the course.

What you cannot do is give up, for the simple reason that *everyone* participates in social activities. Ignoring social media is akin to holding your breath; eventually you'll have to breathe because you'll perish if you don't.

If your organization can develop the capabilities we've described into a repeatable core competence, you will become a social organization. That means you will, as a way of doing business day after day, be able to tap into the vast reservoirs of knowledge, creativity, experience, and passion of all the people your business touches.

Using social media to harvest the collective genius of customers and employees again and again will give your organization an added dimension, one that was lost as it grew in size and complexity. No company, once it's grown, can physically return to the one-office creativity and energy of the start-up we described on the first page of the book. But mass collaboration does provide the potential of regaining some of the innovation, creativity, passion, and engagement of a collaborative startup to address strategic, competitive, and operational challenges.

If your organization isn't learning how to build mass collaboration into the way it works—if you're not becoming a social organization—how will you keep up with competitors that embrace this disruptive opportunity? You and every other manager today must ask: What happens when more and more traditional firms crack the code on mass collaboration and begin to demonstrate the superior capabilities of a social organization?

If you remain unconvinced, read on. In the epilogue, we describe some ways this new capability is likely to develop and the ways people throughout society are starting to use it. Are you ready for a world where the organizational lines within organizations begin to blur and disappear? Are you ready for a world where the lines between your organization and the outside world begin to blur? That's where this is going.

Start the conversation now, engage your people, and be ready for their energy and commitment.

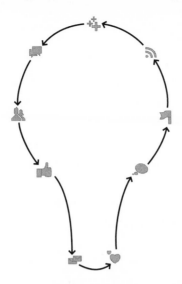

Epilogue
The Social Future

Bob Tobin, a senior manager at a large U.S. government agency, was playing a single-player *Lord of the Rings* video game with his son. The goal is to accumulate points. When it was Bob's turn, his son started giving him pointers and directions for how to beat the game. Bob's initial response was, "You can't help me. That's cheating." His son looked puzzled.

Afterward, they talked about it. His son explained that when he played the game with his friends, they constantly talked him through it with tips and pointers. It was them against the game, not each against the others to get the highest score. And because of that, Bob realized, they conquered the game much more quickly than he could, and faster than any one of them could alone. It was a different mentality about competition.

His other son plays *Call of Duty*, a massively multiplayer online role playing game (MMORPG). He began playing online with people from Ireland, Germany, and South Africa. At first, the others threw jibes at the American boy, but soon they realized he was very good, and they asked him to join their team and compete against other international teams. As a teenager, Bob said, his son was collaborating internationally to meet shared challenges.[1]

For Tobin, his sons' game playing was an epiphany that led him to worry that his federal agency—the entire business world, for that matter—is unprepared to take advantage of the potential that this new generation of people and social technologies offers. He's working now to make sure the agency is ready.

Are you ready? The world is rapidly advancing in its level of social sophistication. If you and your colleagues are working to create a social organization, you'll be well positioned to take advantage of and thrive in the midst of these changes.

Start by examining a potential future where social interactions on a scale never before possible can disrupt the professional world as we know it. As you look at this highly plausible future, consider how a social organization versus a traditional company would operate in this environment.

Social Unions

PatientsLikeMe.com is dedicated to helping patients diagnosed with life-changing diseases. It's creating a new system of medicine by patients for patients. The site says, "We're here to give patients the power to control their disease and to share what they learn with others. To make this happen, we've created a platform for collecting and sharing real world, outcome-based patient data."[2] Patients-LikeMe.com now supports fifteen communities and has enrolled over seventy-thousand patient-members. Over forty thousand unique visitors go to the site every month. And the number of members, visits, and diseases covered is steadily growing. It's hard to imagine a cause people will rally around more powerful than a major illness they all share.

More and more people are congregating on the Web, collecting around common interests and shared goals. But they're very loosely organized—so far. What if, over time, they organize more formally and begin to wield more power? What if collaborative communities become virtual organizations and take on some characteristics of more traditional organizations? How will you respond if their members, in effect, "unionize" and start to exert their collective power and influence on your organization?

We call such a collaborative community—one that actively uses its collective clout to effect social and economic change—a *social union*.

Imagine that PatientsLikeMe.com membership grows to over 70 percent of all people with major diseases in the United States and a large fraction of those in the Americas and Europe. Imagine too that they collectively start endorsing doctors, hospitals, pharmaceuticals, health insurance providers, and the like. Imagine that they start advocating changes in public health policy and endorsing and contributing financially to political candidates. Could they counter the powerful health industry lobby? As a voter or legislator, would you be more sympathetic to the position of PatientsLikeMe.com or the Pharmaceutical Research and Manufacturers of America, a large U.S. firm of lobbyists?

PatientsLikeMe is only one example taken from the fast-expanding universe of collaborative communities on the Web. Imagine such social unions as Soccer Moms, New Mothers, Parents of Children with Mental Illness, Building Contractors, Electronics Purchasers of Europe, Americans for Better Education, Corporate Social Responsibility Worldwide Watch Group—and on and on.

Now go even further and imagine that social unions form inside your own organization. U.S. employment law guarantees the right of employees to gather and discuss the company. What are the issues and problems within your company that might lead people to form social unions and press for change? What if their sentiments leaped the walls of your organization and went public in the larger world? Would that affect your firm's ability to succeed?

At the moment, the social Web is highly disorganized. But it's also still in its infancy. What will happen as it evolves and the new generation that Bob's sons represent moves headlong into the economy? More will join communities. Communities will combine and morph. Some will die as members move to others with more momentum (remember how MySpace, Friendster, and others gave way to Facebook). It's very possible that the Web will end up with fewer communities, but communities with enough critical mass to become social unions able to exert enormous influence—on organizations, governments, society, the world.

Are you prepared for these social unions? Will you need their endorsement to sell your product? Will you sell to communities versus customers? Will you hire a community instead of an employee? Are you preparing to think and act in terms of social unions instead of individuals, markets, and constituents?

Social organizations recognize the power of communities and take a strategic approach to mass collaboration. They maintain an awareness of how social media is changing and integrate it into plans for evolving the company. In working with their own collaborative communities, they've already developed the capability to respond to social unions. They may, in fact, be forming them already. By their nature, social organizations are more vigilant and better prepared for the opportunities and threats just beginning to emerge in the social environment. They can respond significantly faster and with greater impact. They know that if they don't respond quickly, they might as well not respond at all.

Social Swarms

Unlike social unions, which are more organized and long-lived, *social swarms* form quickly around some ephemeral concern and then dissipate with little trace.

An example of this growing trend is Groupon, the "deal-of-the-day" website. Groupon offers an early view into the potential of social swarms, particularly those that span the virtual and physical world. Launched in 2008, Groupon combines elements of social media with online retailing to turn the traditional eBusiness model upside-down. eBusiness models are based on the Internet and its ability to connect large groups of people cheaply to a single integrated supply—think of Amazon. Even with its reseller capability and reviewer ratings, it is still basically an online store.

Groupon, in contrast, uses special offers from local businesses to create a swarm of people around that deal of the day. The power of this approach is its ability to tap into micromarkets by combining mass collaboration with a local interest, a seemingly oxymoronic feat. Groupon sees its ability to proactively create social swarms around local deals as its source of competitive advantage.

In chapter 2 we introduced the idea of collective behavior based on mass coordination. One example we cited took place in the physical world—the Liverpool train station flashdance—and another—@motrinmoms on Twitter—happened only in the virtual world. These kinds of occurrences are just the beginning. Social swarms will become more prevalent and more powerful.

The recent unrest in the Middle East and North Africa offers a glimpse of the possibilities here. The media is right to point out the ease with which social media enables mass movements and transparency. These events would most likely have been impossible without the ability of Facebook, Twitter, and other social media sites to locate people, rally them to a cause, and coordinate their actions.

Our study of mass collaboration and its role in creating social organizations indicates that society is only at the starting point of a model based on universal human values, needs, and rights—freedom of thought, expression, and association; fair recognition of and compensation for the product of one's labor; protection and security; and self-determination. These are the ultimate causes around which people will quickly rally, and they will usher in a new culture of social swarming.

You will have to be fast to respond to swarms. They may make or break your new product launch, decide the local election, kill pending legislation. They may even topple your government. Social organizations with mass collaboration as an integral part of their culture will not only value social swarms but will have experienced them within and outside their organizations. They won't fear the swarms. In many cases, they will *create* the swarms.

The Extended Enterprise

After only eighteen months, Facebook gained and managed five million active users, their "customers," with a staff of only forty. After those eighteen months, Facebook had an estimated market value—based on investments in the site by Microsoft—of over $15 billion, more than GM or Ford. Facebook's value as we write this is an estimated $50 billion.[3] Even if this number is inflated, the value is still significant, to say the least.

Craigslist, with its online classified ads, is a poster child for the kind of leverage building that's possible now. A site with user-generated content and five million visitors per month, Craigslist has significantly disrupted the business model of most U.S. newspapers, which depend heavily on classified ads, and it did this with a total staff of fewer than twenty-five people.[4]

A new leverage champion is a business called PlentyOfFish—a free dating site, as in, "There's plenty of fish in the sea." This service started in British Columbia and has spread into the United States. By 2008, it attracted over 1.4 million unique visitors per month and was making over $10 million dollars per year.[5] Guess how many employees it took to do this? One and a half. The founder worked half-time and had one full-time employee.

How do these social organizations manage to create such value-to-staff leverage? They get the community to do the work for them. The community provides and manages the profiles, content, and interactions. The company facilitates that work, which is what social organizations do. It extends its capabilities through communities. Can your business compete against this increasingly common model? Not if you don't engage the community and get them to do some work for you.

It's easy to dismiss these examples as superficial. Many business leaders discount them by saying, "Well, that's just the Web" or "Our business is different." But dismiss them at your peril—because, as we've shown, more and more traditional brick-and-mortar organizations are already finding innovative ways to apply this leverage-the-community model to extend their business and achieve results otherwise impossible.

It's already happening, and it's just the beginning. What happens when your competitor successfully turns its customer base into an extension of its sales staff? It could, in effect, turn your potential customers into your competitors.

Social media has revived and energized the co-creation movement in which firms engage their customers actively in the design and delivery of products and services. The logic is compelling: people are more likely to buy themselves and recommend to their friends something they had a hand in creating.

What might a competitor that's mastered the skills of co-creation do to your business? If you follow social media, you've certainly heard of Threadless.com, the online T-shirt retailer. It's a much-cited community collaboration–based business where the community it's created designs, chooses, and buys T-shirts before Threadless.com makes and delivers them. Their disruptive goal is that every single T-shirt manufactured makes money. Type "Threadless" into Google and you'll get well over a million hits.

Threadless is also a good example of what we call a *clean-slate competitor*. Such a firm avoids the baggage of a legacy business that, though successful in the past, can inhibit change needed to keep pace with the socialization of business. Clean-slate competitors are not saddled with legacy thinking, inflexible processes, or costly out-of-date technologies. They can capitalize on such new technologies and approaches as community collaboration and cloud computing to compete in new ways. Are you looking out for clean-slate competitors? How will you compete against them?

Are you looking for new ways the community can extend your organization's capabilities? The U.S. Environmental Protection Agency (EPA) has developed a vision for a next-generation system that will help them monitor the health of the earth. Its view is that, if Nike can outfit a running shoe with sensors that analyze a runner's stride, why can't the EPA put a GPS aware sensor on that shoe to measure the levels of lead in the soil?[6] For that matter, why can't it outfit cell phones with sensors that measure air quality and fly-fishing boots to report on the water in our rivers and streams?

By adding social collaboration to this sensing capability—by letting people add local context and even some analysis to their environmental data—the EPA can increase enormously the amount of information available for spotting trends, root causes, and potential solutions. In this vision, every willing outdoor enthusiast would become an EPA researcher, part of a human sensor and analyst network that spans the entire country. Or perhaps an outdoor outfitter like REI or L.L. Bean might participate and expand its business by becoming an environmental force in the world. And, if existing businesses don't do it, a new competitor might arise that does it to gain competitive differentiation.

In short, social organizations are able to do more with less. By capitalizing on communities, they can enjoy greater market impact with fewer resources and investment, and that will produce higher profitability and open up new opportunities.

New Markets and Models

Fliesandfins.com, a fishing community started by Jeremy Cameron, a self-diagnosed fishing fanatic, has over twenty thousand unique visitors a month. Cameron started the community for fun. At the same time he was helping high-end fly fishing, hunting, and sporting goods retailer Orvis with its digital marketing efforts. As the community grew, it attracted Orvis's attention. Orvis and Cameron began talking. Did Orvis want to buy the community? Did it want to strike a partnership? If so, what kind of partnership?[7] Lowe's is in a similar situation with RedAprons.com, a community created by a former Lowe's employee where current employees can discuss all things related to the company. The same thing happened with UPS and browncafe.com.

We're beginning to see a new market emerge around buying, selling, or partnering with collaborative communities. This isn't big Internet or media companies buying large Web platform players like MySpace, YouTube, or Twitter. It's traditional companies buying or partnering with smaller purpose-specific collaborative communities. Are you considering this in your acquisition strategy? Is it part of your growth strategy? Could the reverse happen? Might new competition arise from companies that build communities and backwards integrate? If fliesandfins.com gets big enough, might it buy Orvis?

A social organization with vision and strategy looks for these opportunities and threats. By examining its own business for the potential to create community collaboration, it gains insights into what's possible in its industry. It knows what to look for and target. Finding a collaborative community to buy, partner with, or participate in can be just as effective and often less risky and costly than trying to build your own from scratch.

A new business model for community collaboration is emerging. We're all familiar with the advertising-driven model for social media, such as Facebook; the donation-based model, such as Wikipedia; and the elusive subscription-based model. A new emerging model is the sponsorship-based community.

The Atlantic Media Company in Washington, D.C., launched an exclusive social networking site called 3121, where only members of Congress and their staffs can communicate and collaborate. The name comes from the phone extension—3121—for Capitol Hill. Atlantic Media prepopulated the environment with ten thousand profiles, hoping that participants would take ownership of their profiles and begin networking and collaborating.[8]

This is a model worth noting—because 3121 is a collaboration environment aimed at U.S. Congress employees that is built, managed, and paid for by a private media company, not by the government. It's an indirect funding model—a *sponsorship* funding model. This example represents an opportunity for governments, nonprofits, and NGOs to create collaborative communities without having to make the investment themselves. It also portends a shift in the media industry. Where might you find some partner or other key stakeholder to sponsor a community for your organization?

Some businesspeople are beginning to think social media is close to losing its cachet as the latest, greatest thing. "The last thing the world needs," they think, "is another social media start-up." We think this is a dangerous attitude. Significant innovation in community collaboration will continue from many different directions. Perhaps the buzz will die down, but we're only seeing the tip of the iceberg for social media innovation and change.

Will these and other changes in the market catch you unaware? Will you be a social organization or will you be "outsocialized" by one?

The Age of Mass Transparency

When Anthony's wife was pregnant with their first child, she gave him the list of must-have items they would need when the baby was born. Much to his surprise and consternation, the list included nine different chairs. One was high, one was low, one went in the car, one bounced, one swung side-to-side, one swung back-and-forth, two rocked, and one rolled. After regaining the ability to speak, he said, "I guess we're headed to Babies 'R' Us." "No," she said, "not yet." His wife is not a tech geek by any stretch, but she wouldn't buy any one of these chairs until she went on the Web to find other parents' experiences with each of the products. She would get frustrated if a product didn't provide customer testimonials. "You expect me to buy your product," she would say to the Web page on the screen, "but you can't find anyone to say anything good about it!"

People now expect to find out everything about everything with the click of a mouse or the touch of a fingertip. This is the age of mass transparency.

Social product reviews on the Web certainly aren't new, but they're still rudimentary. Services such as Yelp, SocialYell, and Yahoo! Local are trying to become the preferred information source for rating companies and products. But what if almost everything—people, places, organizations, products, services, events—became a focal point for easy mass collaboration? What if each of those entities had an online profile built and maintained by the masses?

Right now this social information is spotty, disjointed, and difficult to use. But over time that will change. In the United States, we're all familiar with the leading consumer credit rating agencies—FICO, Experian, Equifax, and TransUnion—that create our individual credit scores. Financial institutions use these scores to determine if they will lend money to us and at what interest rate. Imagine similar highly organized and comprehensive services that use information from the masses to give organizations some sort of overall "worthiness score" that helps prospects determine if they're worthy of their business. That overall score might consist of subcategory scores, such as a product-quality score, a customer service score, an environmental friendliness score, a legal score, a regulatory compliance score, and an ethics score. What if the masses help accumulate and organize information on your products and services, your employees and officers, your legal and lobbying activities, your social responsibility record, and even you personally and the business decisions you make?

And imagine these scores are ubiquitous on the Web, mobile devices, and the store shelves, so that people can readily vote with their wallets and change the world one purchase at a time. How would you and your company fare in this scoring? How would you respond to this transparency? Would you issue a press release, or would you mobilize a community? A social organization could do the latter. A social organization will have not only a community collaboration mind-set and culture but an actual portfolio of communities that can be tremendous assets in shaping how the organization is perceived by the world. And how you are perceived by the world is becoming more and more important as people can more readily find and contribute to your reputation.

The world is always changing, but this is a major inflection point. Remember mass production, mass distribution, and mass marketing? Mass collaboration is the next big evolution in business operations. Social organizations that think and operate in terms of community collaboration will thrive in this environment.

Will you be a social organization? Or will you be competing against social organizations? In the next ten years, your ability to evolve into a social organization may determine if you thrive, survive, or disappear.

APPENDIX

Sample Social Media Participation Guidelines

I. Description and definitions

A statement of the context and rationale behind the guidelines.

II. Purpose and Applicability of These Guidelines

Outline the reason for the policy, being clear how these policies complement existing codes of conduct and professionalism.

III. Summary Guidelines for Social Media Participation

A list of the guidelines and a brief description, enabling the reader to see guidelines taken from Gartner's social media policy, include:

Think before you post: Use sound judgment and think about reactions to your post before you post it.

Protect confidential information: Protect our clients' information and information about our business. If in doubt, obtain approval to share the information in social media sites.

Protect and enhance the value of the brand: Present the company in a truthful and fact-based manner. Avoid making derogatory comments about the company, its products, services, employees, or systems.

Be conscious of your online persona: Know when you are representing the company and thus are expected to participate as a professional in a social media environment. If in doubt about when you are representing the company, assume that you are.

IV. Detailed Description of Each Guideline

Building on the summary, provide the details necessary to fully convey the intent of the guideline. For example:

Think before you post: Use sound judgment and think about reactions to your post before you post it. Remember that whatever you post may live for many years on the Web, even after you delete your copy of it. Avoid posting in the heat of the moment, especially in a discussion that is escalating into a "flame" war.

V. Enforcement

Outline the enforcement approaches for these guidelines. Here is a good place to remind participants that their contributions will be monitored and removed if they are in violation of the guidelines, viewed by others as abusive, or otherwise do not contribute to a positive collaborative environment. Members who are employees of the company may face termination, as a violation of these guidelines carries the same weight as violating other company policies. Nonemployee members violating the policy may be blocked and have their contributions removed from the site.

VI. Definition of Permissions, Rights, and Fair Use of the Site Content

It is good practice to remind participants of the nature and fair use of the content generated in the social media site. It is common practice that data created on a site, such as Facebook or Amazon, becomes the property of that site. Sample language includes:

Comments or opinions expressed on this blog are those of the individual contributors only, and do not necessarily represent the views of (the company) Inc. or its management. Readers may copy and redistribute blog postings on other blogs, or otherwise for private, non-commercial or journalistic purposes. This content may not be used for any other purposes in any other formats or media. The content on this blog is provided on an "as-is" basis. The (company) shall not be liable for any damages whatsoever arising out of the content or use of this site.

GLOSSARY

Answer marketplace: A social environment where a participant can pose a question and other participants can contribute and refine answers.[1]

Although answer marketplaces are possible in just about any social media environment, they are specifically designed to facilitate the activity with structures enabling an exchange of value, such as money or points. For example, participants posing a question can offer remuneration for an answer, and answer providers can quote a "price" for their expertise. The two parties can offer and counteroffer. Questioners can review several bids and credentials and choose the most desired one. The process can be public or private (meaning anonymity is managed as part of the marketplace process). Results of the interaction may also be public or private.

Blog: A website designed to make it easy for authors to create entries in chronological order and to facilitate reader commentary on authored entries.

Derived from the term *weblog*, blog entries are displayed in reverse chronological order (most recent entry first) and are generally archived on a periodic basis. Blogs initially were used to express opinions on topical events, such as sports, music, fashion, or politics, but have emerged as established communication channels for businesses as well as for individuals. See *microblogging*.

Collaborative community: A group of individuals who act collectively to pursue a common purpose. A collaborative community is often a diverse group of people, bound by a common cause, from both inside and outside an organization as well as from any level within the organization.

Collective: As a noun, this term reflects the aggregations of people engaged in a shared activity. They may have no direct relationship or even knowledge of one another but are associated through actions around a common cause or concern.

Community collaboration: When a group of people form an indirect relationship (i.e., a community) with one another through support of a common purpose.

Community collaboration is a subset of mass collaboration where members have explicit knowledge that they are collaborating with others in pursuit of a common goal. However, with social media, this nuance is somewhat insignificant, since the vast majority of mass collaboration is community collaboration. In this text, the two terms are often interchangeable.

Crowdsourcing: The processes for sourcing a task or challenge to a broad, distributed set of contributors using the Web and social collaboration techniques.

Crowdsourcing is being successfully applied to narrowly defined tasks, open-ended challenges, or simply a call for ideas. It may also be used internally or externally and, in either case, may be open to any participant or confined to a group of experts. Originally, the term *crowdsourcing* was limited to a "pay for performance" relationship but has evolved to more broad applicability.

Discussion forum: An environment in which participants can pose issues for discussion and respond to any contribution, thus creating *threaded discussions*.

Threaded discussions can spawn a discussion *tree* where the discussion branches out in many directions or subthreads. The participants control the content. This is in contrast to a blog, where the reader comments are limited to a single thread subservient to the blog post and participants can't create a subthread stemming from a comment to the original post.

Emergence: The emergence principle embodies the recognition that you can't predict, model, design, and control mass collaborative interactions and optimize them as you would a fixed business process. Instead, this principle recognizes that an important benefit of the social media environment is that it allows social structures to emerge spontaneously. These structures may be latent or hidden organizational structures, user communities, expertise, work processes, content organization, information taxonomies, and so on.

Emergent structures: Structures that are unknown or unplanned prior to social interactions but that emerge and evolve as activity unfolds.

Emergent structures may be processes, content categorization, organizational networks, and hidden virtual teams. Emergent structures are used to gain a better understanding into the true "nature of things" to more effectively organize, manage, or interact with a community or to optimize its efforts.

Enterprise 2.0: The use of read/write (or Web 2.0 technologies) by businesses for a business purpose.

The term *enterprise 2.0* was coined by Andrew McAfee's *Enterprise 2.0: New Collaborative Tools for Your Organization's Toughest Challenges* (Boston: Harvard Business School Press, 2009).

Expertise location: Identifying human expertise, determining the status of that resource, and integrating the person or expertise into the interaction process. It is used to maintain in-depth representations of skills, geographic locations, availability, and other parameters relevant to the use of the expertise.

Folksonomy: *See* social tagging.

Gamification: Gamification is the application of game theory and mechanics to non-game activities to motivate desired behaviors.

Grassroots community: A type of collaborative community that emerges on its own, either within or outside of the organization's collaborative tools. Grassroots communities represent a bottom-up approach to organizing community-based collaboration. As they form, the organization applies the No, Go, Grow decision model to determine the appropriate level of organizational support and investment.

Idea engine: A social environment in which participants can enter an idea for social validation and contribution.

Other participants can support and augment the idea, ignore it, or refute it. Like answer marketplaces, idea engines are designed specifically to enable mass collaboration around ideas so that the best, most supported, and most viable ideas are vetted and advanced by the collective. In some cases, idea engines operate like a stock exchange, where participants are able to invest in ideas and then get a return on that investment if an idea moves forward in the vetting process.

Independence: A characteristic of mass collaboration that allows participation anytime, anyplace, and for any member. The independence principle captures the requirement for collaborative communities to choose the way of working that best fits their purpose and the fact that social media does not require workflow mechanisms that might undermine collaboration.

Mass collaboration: The ability for multitudes of people to quickly and effectively contribute to the development or evolution of an idea, artifact, process, plan, action, and so on.

In the context of social software, mass collaboration includes participation by people who may not otherwise have had a preexisting relationship. Examples of mass collaboration include social networking, social tagging/folksonomies, crowdsourcing, and idea engines.

Microblogging: A narrow-scope form of blogging.

Pioneered by the social network site Twitter, microblogging users publish very short, often one-line messages to their contacts, who have specifically opted to follow the blogger's microblogging activities. This is a *one-to-many* approach to short communications where the "many" choose whom to follow, versus *one-to-one* or *one-to-few* short communications, such as texting, where the recipients are chosen by the sender.

No, Go, Grow decision model: A systematic way of determining if and how a community collaboration effort should move forward. The decision framework is applied during development of the collaboration strategy as well as whenever the organization needs to make a determination regarding grass roots communities.

Participation: One of the six principles of mass collaboration. The participation principle recognizes the importance of generating contributions and feedback from the collaborative community via social media.

Persistence: With social media, participant contributions are captured and stored for others to view, share, comment on, and augment. Persistence differentiates social media from synchronous conversational interactions, where much of the information exchanged is either lost or captured only in part, as an additional writing or recording activity.

Prediction market: A mechanism that can forecast outcomes of ongoing issues of contention or uncertain outcomes, based on analysis of content or actions taken by the collective.

Prediction markets rely on crowdsourcing. They can also be used to prioritize ideas (users bet on which ideas have the greatest chance of success) and to assess risk (users bet on which paths carry the least risk).

Presence: A foundational technology that provides indications of the status and availability of contacts.

Presence shows whether a participant is online, and may provide a description of that person's status. While presence is often used by applications in nonsocial environments (e.g., e-mail or instant messaging), it is increasingly used by social solutions to show the current status of a community's participants.

Purpose: A specific and meaningful reason for collaboration that will motivate members of a community to interact and contribute. The purpose is the reason why individuals voluntarily join a collaborative community and why the organization is interested in supporting mass collaboration.

Purpose roadmap: A set of related and sequenced purposes that define how the community's collaboration can start, grow, and evolve. The roadmap is predominantly a planning tool that provides a means to assess the community's progress and influence its activities and priorities.

Social badge: A social badge is an icon given to a social media participant in recognition of some behavior or accomplishment. Badges can be for positive or negative behaviors and may come with some reward or disincentive. Badges often accompany participation "levels" achieved.

Social bookmarking: Social bookmarking is social media functionality allowing users to share, evaluate, comment on, tag, organize, search, and manage bookmark links of web resources.

Social computing: An approach to IT whereby individuals tailor information-based and collaborative technologies to support interactions with relatively large and often loosely defined groups.

Social computing is an umbrella term that describes individuals' increasing use of technology for the purpose of participating in group activities (which may be in the execution of work-related activities). Social computing extends the reach, scope, and number of relationships in which individuals can actively engage and amplifies each individual voice so he or she can potentially reach global audiences and communities. It is fundamentally different from enterprise computing, which is a planned, governed, and controlled architecture designed to meet the specific functional needs of an enterprise in the pursuit of business activities (or of a public-sector organization in the delivery of services). It is also different from personal computing, which centers on individuals using computing technologies for individual productivity versus group activities.

Social CRM: Social applications intended for sales, marketing, and customer service organizations to engage customers or prospects along any CRM process.

Social CRM is used to engage customers in a range of collaborative activities, including codeveloping of new products or services, generating brand awareness, offering price comparisons, assisting the selling process, or connecting with post purchase activities (such as customer service), as well as marketing support for post-purchase dissonance.

Social feedback: The ability for participants in a social media environment to add their opinions about the quality or relevance of the content.

Common examples of social feedback are like/not like, thumbs up/thumbs down, dig it, star ratings, social commentary, tagging (or mass categorization), flagging, and badging.

Social media: An online environment opened for the purposes of mass collaboration where all invited participants can create, post, rate, enhance, discover, consume, and share content without a direct intermediary.

The term *media* in this context is a collaboration environment characterized by storage and transmission of messages around or about content, while *social* describes the distinct way these messages propagate in a many-to-many fashion among peers. Mass collaboration is enabled by and conducted through social media.

Social network analysis: A technique for analyzing patterns of relationships among people in groups.

It is useful for examining the social structure and interdependencies of individuals or organizations. It involves collecting data from multiple sources (such as surveys, e-mails, blogs, and other electronic artifacts), analyzing the data to identify relationships, and mining it for new information, such as the quality or effectiveness of the relationship.

Social networking: The act of establishing online many-to-many human connections for the purposes of sharing information with the network or subsets thereof. Although one-to-one connections are possible in social network sites, the preponderance of activity engages a broader range of participants in any given network.

Social organization: A social organization is an organization with a competency in strategically applying mass collaboration to business challenges and opportunities. An organization becomes a social organization by learning from repeated success in using social media to form collaborative communities that deliver significant business value.

Social profile: A description of individuals' salient characteristics that meaningfully identify them for a given social site or for a collaboration application.

Profiles describe any number of characteristics about individuals, such as interests, expertise, professional affiliations, status, recent activity, and geographic location. Individuals may also use their social profile to determine privacy, access, and other preferences for social activity.

Social publishing: The capability for the masses to accumulate their individually developed content (versus shared development via a wiki) into a usable repository and shared environment for social use and feedback. Individually developed content is different from content that is collaboratively developed, as in a wiki. Common examples include photographs and video.

Social software: Software that enables, captures, and organizes interaction between participants in a social site or solution.

The ability for social software to enable mass collaboration differentiates it from other collaboration technologies. Examples of social software include the technologies that enable blogs, wikis, discussion forums, expertise location, and many other technologies.

Social tagging: User-defined metadata that can serve to organize socially contributed content.

Also known as *folksonomies*, social tagging evolves when many users identify their classification of a given content element. *Tag clouds* pinpoint various identifiers and the frequency of use on a folksonomy site. This type of grassroots community classification is an example of collective intelligence providing emergent structure to a socially accumulated body of content.

Social technologies: Any technology that facilitates social interactions and is enabled by a communications capability, such as the Internet or a mobile device.

Examples of social technologies are social software (e.g., wikis, blogs, social networks) and communication capabilities (e.g., Web conferencing) that are targeted at and enable social interactions.

Social Web: The universe of opportunities available for people (the general public) to actively participate in open group activities on the Web. The social Web is generally considered the human social aspect of Web 2.0.

Transparency: The ability of all participants in a collaborative community to see each other's contributions. One of the six principles of mass collaboration, transparency gives the community the information needed to self-organize, self-govern, self-correct and evolve.

Virtual world: A virtual world is a real-time, 3D online community environment where users create avatars to interact with one another and collaborate to use and create a variety of simulated objects.

Web 2.0: The evolution of the Web from a collection of hyperlinked content pages to a platform for human collaboration and system development and delivery.

Technologies that enable Web 2.0 include Ajax and Really Simple Syndication (RSS), as well as overall concepts such as social media, Web platforms, and Web-oriented architecture.

Wiki: A collaborative authoring system for creating and maintaining linked collections of Web pages.

A wiki enables users to add or change pages in a Web browser without having to worry about where and how the content is stored. Wikis enable mass authorship—potentially millions of people can collaborate to generate new content.

NOTES

Chapter 1

1. Anthony J. Bradley, "Five Major Challenges Organizations Face Regarding Social Software," Gartner Inc., February 15, 2008.

2. Kevin Cooney and Chris Wire, Xilinx Inc., telephone conversations with Mark P. McDonald on February 5, 2010, and October 14, 2010.

3. FICO and myFICO are trademarks of the Fair Isaac Corporation in the United States and other countries.

4. Adam Sarner, "The Business Impact of Social Computing: Real-World Results for Marketing," Gartner Inc., November 13, 2009.

5. Mark P. McDonald and Dave Aron, "Reimagining IT: The 2011 CIO Agenda," Gartner Inc., January 1, 2011.

6. Todd Nissen, Ford Motor Company, e-mails with Anthony J. Bradley, May 19–30, 2011.

7. Anthony J. Bradley, "The Business Impact of Social Computing: Real-World Results for Customer Engagement," Gartner Inc., November 4, 2009.

8. Miguel Lozano, CEMEX Inc., telephone conversations with Mark P. McDonald, September 27, 2010, and January 5, 2011.

9. Gilberto Garcia, CEMEX Inc., telephone conversations with Mark P. McDonald on September 27, 2010, and January 5, 2011.

10. Miguel Lozano, CEMEX Inc., telephone conversations with Mark P. McDonald on September 27, 2010, and January 5, 2011.

Chapter 2

1. The terms *social media*, *community*, and *purpose* are used in many different ways by various writers about social media. We define these terms specifically for what we mean by them in the context of this book (see the glossary at the end of this book).

2. Nicholas Carlson, "At Last—The Full Story of How Facebook Was Founded," *Business Insider*, March 5, 2010.

3. Joe Wrighter, "How Craigslist Started," *Helium*, March 22, 2007, http://www.helium.com/items/225319-how-craigslist-started.

4. Nisan Gabbay, "MySpace Case Study: Not a Purely Viral Start," *Startup Review*, September 10, 2006, http://www.startup-review.com/blog/myspace-case-study-not-a-purely-viral-start.php.

5. Anthony J. Bradley, "The Six Core Principles of Social-Media-Based Collaboration," Gartner Inc., December 10, 2009.

6. Miguel Lozano and Gilberto Garcia, CEMEX Inc., telephone conversation with Mark P. McDonald on September 29, 2010.

7. Anthony J. Bradley, "Employing Social Media for Business Impact: Key Collective Behavior Patterns," Gartner Inc., February 3, 2011.

8. Carol Rozwell, "Five Case Study Examples of Social Network Analysis," Gartner Inc., August 27, 2008.

9. Traffic statistics from compete.com as of May 20, 2011.

10. http://bookclubs.barnesandnoble.com/t5/help/faqpage/faq-category-id/participation#participation.

11. Bill Marriot, "Marriot on the Move," February 22, 2011, http://www.blogs.marriott.com/.

12. Miguel Lozano, CEMEX Inc., telephone conversation with Mark P. McDonald on September 29, 2010.

Chapter 4

1. NASA MSFC Social Media Strategy Workshop, sponsored by Jonathan Pettus, NASA MSFC CIO, facilitated by Anthony J. Bradley, Gartner Inc., July 29, 2009.

2. Jonathan Pettus, NASA MSFC, telephone conversation with Anthony J. Bradley on May 11, 2011.

3. Anthony J. Bradley, "How to Assess the Suitability of Social Media for Enterprise Collaboration Scenarios," Gartner, Inc., October 9, 2009.

4. Anthony J. Bradley, "An Examination of 200 Successful Social Media Implementations," Gartner, Inc., June 15, 2011.

5. Michael Smith, "The Gartner Business Value Model: A Framework for Measuring Business Performance," Gartner Inc., March 26, 2010.

6. Anthony J. Bradley, "The Business Impact of Social Computing on Company Governance," Gartner, Inc., September 11, 2008.

7. NASA MSFC Social Media Strategy Workshop.

Chapter 5

1. U.S. Environmental Protection Agency, "Watershed Central Community," April 8, 2011, http://www.epa.gov/watershedcentral/.

2. Anthony J. Bradley and Nikos Drakos, "Seven Key Characteristics of a Good Purpose for Social Software," Gartner Inc., July 24, 2008.

3. Anthony J. Bradley, "Use a Gartner Governance Model to More Safely Empower Grassroots Social Media Efforts," Gartner Inc., October 9, 2009.

4. Anthony J. Bradley, "12 Criteria to Assess Grassroots Risk and Potential in Social Media Solutions," Gartner Inc., October 9, 2009.

5. Mary Brandel, "The New Employee Connection: Social Networking Behind the Firewall," *Computerworld*, August 11, 2008.

6. Procter & Gamble, "BeingGirl: for Girls by Girls," http://www. beinggirl.com.

7. Massimo Calabresi, "Wikipedia for Spies: The CIA Discovers Web 2.0," *Time*, April 8, 2009.

Chapter 6

1. Anthony J. Bradley, "Toolkit: Employing a Purpose Road Map to Build and Execute a Social-Media Strategy," Gartner Inc., November 4, 2009.

2. BlueCross BlueShield of Tennessee is an independent licensee of the Blue-Cross BlueShield Association.

3. BCBST Social Media Strategy Workshop, sponsored by Trevin Bernarding, Director, eBusiness Development, BCBST, facilitated on March 22, 2010, by Anthony J. Bradley, Gartner Inc.

4. Trevin Bernarding, BCBST, telephone conversation with Anthony J. Bradley on May 2, 2011.

5. Barry Paperno and Lynn Johnson, FICO Inc., telephone conversation with Anthony J. Bradley on May 5, 2011.

Chapter 7

1. Peer Connect Workshop, sponsored by Nir Polonsky, Gartner Inc., facilitated by Anthony J. Bradley, September 15, 2010.

2. Anthony J. Bradley, "Ten Primary Design Considerations for Delivering Social Software Solutions: The PLANT SEEDS Framework," Gartner Inc., July 13, 2009.

3. Paul Price, Acosta, telephone conversation with Anthony J. Bradley on May 5, 2011.

4. Acosta Social Media Strategy Workshop, sponsored by Paul Price, Executive Vice President, Marketing Services, Acosta, facilitated by Anthony J. Bradley, Gartner Inc., on August 17, 2010.

5. Nisan Gabbay, "MySpace Case Study: Not a Purely Viral Start," *Startup Review*, September 10, 2006, http://www.startup-review.com/blog/myspace-case-study-not-a-purely-viral-start.php.

6. Charles Arthur, "What Is the 1% rule?," *The Guardian*, July 20, 2006.

7. Malcolm Gladwell, *The Tipping Point: How Little Things Make a Big Difference* (Boston: Little, Brown and Company, 2000).

Chapter 8

1. Denis Self and Michael Cuthrell, Electronic Arts Inc., telephone conversations with Mark P. McDonald on October 12, 2009, and March 7, 2011.

2. Mark Brewer, Seagate Technologies, telephone conversation with Mark P. McDonald on November 30, 2010.

3. Kevin Cooney and Chris Wire, Xilinx Inc., telephone conversations with Mark P. McDonald on February 5, 2010, and October 14, 2010.

4. Miguel Lozano, CEMEX Inc., telephone conversations with Mark P. McDonald on January 5, 2011, and March 23, 2011.

5. Denis Self and Michael Cuthrell, Electronic Arts., telephone conversations with Mark P. McDonald on October 12, 2009, and March 7, 2011.

Chapter 9

1. Gilberto Garcia and Miguel Lozano, CEMEX Inc., telephone conversation with Mark P. McDonald on March 23, 2011.

2. Paul Kay, Univita, telephone conversation with Mark P. McDonald and Anthony Bradley on November 23, 2010.

3. Gilberto Garcia and Miguel Lozano, CEMEX Inc., telephone conversation with Mark P. McDonald, March 23, 2011.

4. Mitch Steward, e-mail sent to supporters on November 13, 2011.

Chapter 10

1. Susan Malish, Loyola University Chicago, telephone conversation and e-mails with Mark P. McDonald on April 7, 2011; Mark P. McDonald, "Loyola University Chicago: Creating the Foundation of Committed Communities," Gartner Inc., March 26, 2010.

2. Gilberto Garcia and Miguel Lozano, CEMEX Inc., telephone conversations with Mark P. McDonald on September 27, 2010, January 5, 2011, and March 23, 2011.

3. Gilberto Garcia and Miguel Lozano, CEMEX Inc., telephone conversations with Mark P. McDonald, September 27, 2010.

4. http://www.nbcconnecticut.com/news/local/Facebook-Posts-Cost-Windsor-Locks-Superintendent-His-Job-103014819.html.

5. Eric Frazier, "Facebook Post Costs Waitress Her Job," Charlotte Observer, May 17, 2010, http://www.charlotteobserver.com/2010/05/17/1440447/ facebook-post-costs-waitress-her.html.

6. Evann Gastaldo, "3 Teachers Fired for Flirting with Students on Facebook," Newser, October 18, 2010, http://www.newser.com/story/103180/3-teachers-fired-for-flirting-with-students-on-facebook.html.

7. http://www.facebook.com/group.php?gid=63470796208.

8. You can access an interesting compendium of publicly available social media policy documentation at http://socialmediagovernance.com/policies.php; see also Gartner's social media guidelines, coauthored by Anthony J. Bradley and Nick Gall, which the company makes available on its blog network at www .blogs/gartner.com.

9. Kevin Cooney and Chris Wire, Xilinx, telephone conversations with Mark P. McDonald on February 5, 2010, and October 14, 2010; and Mark P. McDonald, "Xilinx: Consumerization, Community and Capability Using Web 2.0," Gartner Inc., February 24, 2010.

10. Gilberto Garcia and Miguel Lozano, CEMEX Inc., telephone conversations with Mark P. McDonald on January 5, 2011, and March 23, 2011.

11. Mark Brewer, Seagate Technologies., telephone conversation with Mark P. McDonald on November 30, 2010.

12. Gilberto Garcia and Miguel Lozano, CEMEX Inc., telephone conversations with Mark P. McDonald on January 5, 2011, and March 23, 2011.

Epilogue

1. Bob Tobin, meeting with Anthony J. Bradley on March 24, 2009.

2. http://www.patientslikeme.com/about.

3. Susanne Craig and Andrew Ross Sorkin, "Goldman Offering Clients a Chance to Invest in Facebook," *New York Times*, January 2, 2011.

4. Del Jones, "Can Small Businesses Help Win the War?," *USAToday*, January 1, 2007.

5. Randall Stross, "From 10 Hours a Week, $10 Million a Year," *New York Times*, January 13, 2008.

6. U.S. Environmental Protection Agency, "Global Earth Observation System of Systems (GEOSS)," http://www.epa.gov/geoss/ami/.

7. Jeremy Cameron, meeting with Anthony J. Bradley on March 8, 2011.

8. Anthony J. Bradley, "A New Model for Funding Social Media," Gartner blog network, September 29, 2009.

Glossary

1. This glossary is based on Susan Landry and Anthony J. Bradley, *Social Simplified: Gartner's Glossary of Social Technologies and Terms* (Stamford, CT: Gartner Inc., 2010).

INDEX

Note: Page numbers followed by *f* refer to figures; page numbers followed by *t* refer to tables; page numbers followed by *n* refer to notes.

ACKNOWLEDGMENTS

This book started as two separate projects. One focused on an approach for organizations to foster mass collaboration using social media, and the other concentrated on social media's impact on management. It immediately became clear that social media's importance and impact on organizations was greater, and we quickly realized that a book with a dual focus—on both the organization and management—would present a practical and comprehensive approach for managers seeking to maximize success with social media.

This book would not have been possible without the talents and contributions of Kent Lineback and Heather Pemberton Levy, who were essential in helping us organize our thoughts as we put the book together. Kent, we want to thank you for your invaluable collaboration, your constant focus on the reader, and for helping us bring a manager's perspective to what many consider a technology issue. This book would not be what it is without your dedication and your insight. Heather, thank you for guiding this project through the creation and publication process and for your constant support and coaching. Thanks also to Peter Sondergaard and Dale Kutnick for their support and early recognition of the potential of this book, their belief in the project, and for recognizing the flexibility we both needed to carry it out. We would also like to recognize Andrew Spender, who has championed this project and its ambitious goals. Finally, we'd like to express our thanks to Jeff Kehoe and Kathleen Carr at Harvard Business Review Press for their valuable support and editorial insights.

A book on social media is nothing without the shared experiences of the organizations and leaders who are championing community collaboration in their firms. While many are quoted in the book, we specifically want to thank the following people for their time and energy in sharing their social media experiences with us: Paul Price at Acosta, Trevin Bernarding at BCBST, Miguel Angel Lozano Martinez and Jesus Gilberto Garcia at CEMEX, Dennis Self and Michael Cuthrell at Electronic Arts, Robert Tobin at the Federal Aviation Administration, Barry Paperno at FICO, Nir Polonsky at Gartner, Susan Malisch at Loyola University Chicago, Jonathan Pettus at NASA MSFC, Jeremy Cameron at Simple Solutions, Mark Brewer at Seagate Technology, Paul Kay at Univita Health, and Kevin Cooney and Chris Wire at Xilinx.

—Anthony J. Bradley and Mark P. McDonald

I want to thank my wife Renee for the many nights and weekends she had to manage the children and run the household without my help. I would also like to thank Robert Deshaies and Susan Landry for their help in reviewing early drafts. Their feedback was highly valuable. Gartner has a strong team of analysts covering social media, and my research in this area over the past four years, including many of the concepts in this book, has benefited greatly from their guidance. Special thanks to Tom Austin, Nikos Drakos, Jeff Mann, Carol Rozwell, and Adam Sarner.

Finally, since this may be my one and only book, I'd like to express my gratitude to Valentin Sribar, Dale Kutnick, and Nick Gall for their overall positive impact on my career and professional growth.

—Anthony J. Bradley, San Antonio, Texas

It takes a social network to write a book on social media, and while there are many people to acknowledge and many whom I will undoubtedly miss, I would like to thank a few people in particular who contributed to the development of the ideas in this book. My personal thanks go to my family—Carolyn, Brian, and Sarah—who provided constant support and perceptive comments. My professional thanks go to my colleagues at Gartner, whose interest and dialogue have sharpened these ideas; in particular Richard Hunter, who has encouraged this project. Peter Keen, you will notice the transition from a value network to a social network in this book—thank you for your constant support. Thanks also to Peter Weill, Jeanne Ross, and Stephanie Woerner at MIT CISR for a continued open exchange of ideas, and Jeannie Harris for sharing ideas. Thanks to my colleagues in Gartner's Executive Programs for the honor of sharing new ideas with their members. Finally, my thanks to the executives who are members of our Executive Programs; working with you is an ongoing privilege, and you have my deep appreciation for sharing your issues and your experiences. Your willingness to do something different is an inspiration to all of us.

—Mark McDonald, St. Charles, Illinois

ABOUT THE AUTHORS

Anthony J. Bradley is a Group Vice President at Gartner, Inc. and a lead analyst for social media and Web 2.0. He spearheaded the creation of and now leads Gartner's analyst blogosphere. He also participated in the design of Gartner's Peer Connect social media community. He has been building and investigating mass collaboration for over fifteen years. Before joining Gartner, as cofounder and Chief Technology Officer of Appergy Inc., he developed several mass collaboration products. Anthony led META Group's Digital Products Division, responsible for delivering collaborative solutions for clients to execute on change initiatives using META Group content. With Booz Allen Hamilton, Anthony worked on several social media projects including a design alternative for Army Knowledge Online (AKO). He has an MBA in information technology from the Merage School of Business at the University of California, Irvine, and an undergraduate degree from the U.S. Naval Academy. You can continue to follow his thoughts on social media at blogs.gartner.com/anthony_bradley.

Mark P. McDonald is a Group Vice President and Fellow at Gartner, Inc., where he works with executive teams on applying social and other technologies to achieve business results. Prior to working for Gartner, he was a partner with Accenture, responsible for the Center for Process Excellence. He holds a PhD in technology policy management from TU Delft, Netherlands, and a master's degree in economics and international finance from Trinity College in Hartford,

Connecticut. He is coauthor, with Peter Keen, of *The eProcess Edge*. He is an active blogger and has been published or interviewed by the *Wall Street Journal*, *Forbes Online*, the *Financial Times*, and CNBC. You can continue to follow Mark's thoughts on social media, management, and technology at blogs.gartner.com/mark_mcdonald.